P9-AOX-118

The Sacraments

An Exploration into Their
Meaning and Practice in the
RLDS Church

The Sacraments

An Exploration into Their Meaning and Practice in the RLDS Church

Revised Edition
by
Peter A. Judd

Temple Worship Center
Reorganized Church of Jesus Christ
of Latter Day Saints

Herald Publishing House

This edition is a revised, updated version of *The Sacraments: An Exploration into Their Meaning and Practice in the Saints Church* (Independence, Missouri: Herald Publishing House, 1978). All rights reserved. No part of the text may be reproduced in any form without written permission of the author, except brief quotations used in connection with reviews in magazines or newspapers.

Copyright © 1992
Herald Publishing House
Independence, Missouri
Printed in the United States of America

Library of Congress Cataloging-in-Publication Data
Judd, Peter A., 1943-
    The Sacraments : an Exploration into Their Meaning and
Practice in the RLDS Church / by Peter A. Judd.—Rev. ed.
        p.   cm.
    Includes bibliographical references.
    ISBN 0-8309-0624-X
    1. Sacraments—Reorganized Church of Jesus Christ of
Latter Day Saints. 2. Reorganized Church of Jesus Christ
of Latter Day Saints—Doctrines. I. Title.
BX8675.J827   1992
234'.16—dc20   92-28306
                                                          CIP

95 94 93   2 3 4

Table of Contents

Preface

Over the last thirty years the Reorganized Church of Jesus Christ of Latter Day Saints has participated in some significant struggles as part of the ongoing task of reevaluation of its mission, priorities, and practices. Reevaluation is a necessary part of the process of restoration. It is in keeping with the admonition: "Instruction which has been given in former years is applicable in principle to the needs of today and should be so regarded by those who are seeking to accomplish the will of their heavenly Father. But the demands of a growing church require that these principles shall be evaluated and subjected to further interpretation."*

As a result of this process of self-examination, the church now sees itself more in terms of its role in the world as an agent of God's redemptive ministry than before. The church has come to appreciate the heritage and common mission it shares with other Christian denominations. This appreciation, however, must always be kept in balance with a growing understanding of our identity as Reorganized Latter Day Saints.

Concern for distinctiveness exists side by side with concern for those aspects of belief and practice shared in common with other Christians. Both concerns are equally valid. Overemphasis on either at the expense of the other distorts the church's perception of its calling and seriously reduces its effectiveness as God's instrument of ministry.

The sacraments have always been an important mark of identity in the RLDS Church. The practice and the

---

*Doctrine and Covenants 147:7

7

meaning attached to them bear both similarities and differences to the sacraments of other Christian denominations. In a time of exploration and examination it is appropriate to explore the role of the sacraments in the church. This book is written with that intent in mind. The approach is to explore the practice and meaning of the sacraments in the church today. The scriptural basis for the practice and interpretation of each sacrament is presented and significant changes in procedure and understanding are described.

For each of the sacraments several meanings are presented. These all have validity and are not suggested as alternatives which exclude each other. Some meanings have received varying emphases in the church over the years. Others have not but are presented as additional interpretations to consider.

Six of the eight sacraments of the church are practiced in public worship settings. For each of these sacraments suggestions are provided for the ordering of the service of worship. The worship suggestions included in this book are specific in nature and apply to services of worship in which the sacraments are celebrated. General worship helps are not included but are available elsewhere. For sources of general worship materials write to the Temple Worship Center, P.O. Box 1059, Independence, MO 64051. It is hoped that the worship suggestions included in this book will assist the church in the task of elevating the sacraments to a more dignified and meaningful place in the life of the church in general and in its worship in particular. This is timely in light of the recent inspired counsel presented to the church in April 1992: "Look especially to the sacraments to enrich the spiritual life of the body. Seek for greater understanding of my purpose in these sacred rites and prepare to receive a renewed confirmation of the presence of my Spirit in your experiences of worship."*

This book is not designed as a procedural manual for ministers who officiate in the sacraments of the church. Procedural details are included only as they bear on the basic practice and meaning of the sacraments. Individuals who need additional information on procedural matters are referred to the latest edition of *The Priesthood Manual* available from Herald House and office-centered courses offered by the church's Temple School Center.

This work is primarily addressed to the adult membership of the RLDS Church. It is hoped the material contained in this book will interest priesthood and others involved in the practice of the sacraments and the planning of the worship services that provide their context. However, anyone involved in inquiry into the life and mission of the church in the present day may find this book useful.

This book is appropriate for study in a church school setting and by priesthood and other groups in the church. Questions for individual or group study and activity suggestions are found at the end of each of the nine chapters. In most cases more activities and questions are included than will be used by a class. This necessitates a teacher or the class as a whole deciding which ones to use. The activities and questions are not printed in any particular order. Choices should be made based on the needs and interests of the group involved.

Many colleagues and friends within the RLDS Church have influenced the content of this book. I extend

_____
*Doctrine and Covenants 158:11c

9

special appreciation to Paul Jones, professor of theology at Saint Paul School of Theology, who had a unique influence on this work. The research and writing were in large part done as a directed study under his guidance and encouragement.

This revised edition includes updated information and insights while preserving the approach of the first edition and the research on which it was based. Scripture quotations are from the Inspired Version of the Bible (IV) and from the 1966 edition of the Book of Mormon unless otherwise indicated. Where the Inspired Version versification differs from that of other versions, it is indicated in parentheses following the citation.

Consistent with the continuing mood of inquiry in the church, this book is designed to raise questions rather than to answer them. More research and inquiry remain to be done. It is my hope that this work can serve as a stimulus to others to pursue such endeavors.

Peter A. Judd

CHAPTER 1

The Sacraments and the Church

Sacrament and Sacraments

The concept of sacrament is closely related to that of revelation—an important principle in the life of the RLDS Church. Sacrament has to do with the expression of God's self within the human experience. Some writers have viewed Jesus Christ as the primary sacrament because in the Son, God is most fully revealed. Others have extended this principle a step further by viewing the church—in its several, varied denominational and historical expressions—also as sacrament. The Apostle Paul referred to the church as Christ's body, or in other words the present-day expression in human form of Christ just as Christ was the incarnation (expression in human form) of God.

The ritual acts the church refers to as sacraments can then be seen as the next step: the specific actions of the gathered "body." It may be helpful to see the sacraments of the church as linked to God via the church and Christ as follows: God→Christ→church→sacraments, each being the successive and more tangible expression of the one preceding it.

From the earliest years of Christianity the church has used these special rites called sacraments to mark its identity, celebrate its unity, and symbolize its mission. Sacraments have always been basic to the corporate life of Christians. As the years passed Christianity divided into denominations. With this division variations emerged in the number of sacraments, in their meaning and importance, and in the way they were performed. Baptism and the Lord's Supper are most universally accepted as sacraments. Others such as confirmation, ordination, and marriage are regarded by many Christian denominations as sacraments. In addition to these five, the blessing of children, administration to the sick, and the evangelist's blessing are accepted as sacraments by the RLDS Church.

Characteristics of Sacraments

Each sacrament has its own unique characteristics and will be explored in subsequent chapters. It is possible, however, to identify a number of elements that are shared by several or all sacraments. These characteristics are not equally evident nor do they receive equal emphasis in each sacrament. Nevertheless they are all important to an understanding of sacraments in general and each sacrament in particular.

First, the sacraments are vehicles of God's ACTION and REVELATION in the lives of human beings. Reorganized Latter Day Saints have always been strong believers in God's self-revelation to humanity in all ages. Specifically the church has maintained that God called it into existence to participate in the divine mission to redeem the world. This characteristic of sacraments is widely accepted throughout Christianity but variously interpreted. On one extreme is the view that the sacraments are the highest form of God's action and self-revealment. On the other extreme is the view that all of creation evidences God's action. According to this latter view, sacraments express God's action but only in the same way as the whole created order. A moderate view would suggest that the sacraments are a unique, but not exclusive, medium of God's action. The power of God in the sacraments is suggested in Doctrine and Covenants 83:3c, which indicates that in the ordinances (sacraments) "the power of godliness is manifest."

Second, in the sacraments Christ is present. Christ's presence in the world as Jesus of Nazareth is the universal testimony of Christians in all times and places. Yet Christians also affirm that Christ is ever-living. This is the testimony of the resurrection, that God raised Jesus to new life, never again to be subject to death. In the sacraments Christ's ever-living presence is made known and experienced. This presence is the continuing assurance and experience of Emmanuel (God with us). In the sacraments we are made aware once again that God did not desert humanity at Calvary. Instead, God in Christ comes forth to be with us again and again in the same way that Jesus came forth from the tomb.

Third, in the sacraments the church is renewed. The church is called to perform Christ's work and ministry in the world. As such, it is indeed Christ's body. The sacraments provide occasions where, through the action of God and the presence of Christ, the church is commissioned again and renewed by its founder and head. The sacraments sustain the church so it can continue to act as Christ's presence in the world. Without Christ's presence in the sacraments the church could not function as his presence in the world.

Fourth, the sacraments are expressions of the covenant relationship between God and humanity. In the sacraments God's faithfulness and unending love are reaffirmed and made evident. God chooses us anew and extends to us the opportunity to join in the divine mission of redeeming the world. The sacraments are also the vehicles of human response to the divine initiative and call. They provide us with the opportunity to give ourselves in allegiance to God and to take upon ourselves the name of Christ. God reaches out to covenant with us and invites us to covenant in return. The sacraments serve to reaffirm and solidify the covenant that gives the church its identity and sustenance.

Fifth, the sacraments are performed in response to Christ's instruction. An important base of authority for the practice of sacraments in the church is Jesus' instruction and practice as recorded in the testimony of the Gospel writers. Sacraments based on Jesus' action (e.g., the Lord's Supper) and those understood to be commanded by him (e.g., baptism) are given high priority in the various Christian denominations' lists of sacraments. Others (e.g., marriage) are not universally accepted as sacraments.

The scriptural record is, however, subject to varied interpretation. It may seem obvious to Latter Day Saints that the blessing of children and healing were, according to the biblical record, practiced by Jesus himself. Yet few other denominations practice the blessing of children or administration to the sick.

Sixth, the sacraments provide opportunity for remembering Christ. As the foundation and head of the church, Christ and his ministry need to be constantly remembered and relived by the church. The remembrance aspect of the sacraments is particularly evident in the Lord's Supper where Jesus is recorded as saying, "This do in remembrance of me."[1] Through the sacraments the church remembers Jesus' birth, ministry, crucifixion, and resurrection. Human beings repeatedly forget how, at great cost, God sent Christ to the world as a free and undeserved gift. In the sacraments is found the constant reminder we need so much.

Seventh, the sacraments are acts of obedience to God. As servants of Christ, members of the church participate in the sacraments as expressions of allegiance to and obedience to the purposes of God. The divine intent is that human beings will live in harmonious fellowship with each other and grow toward individual and corporate fulfillment in the image of God. The sacraments provide the vehicles whereby we can offer ourselves in submission to this divine intent. In the RLDS tradition sacraments are frequently called "ordinances." The use of this term is expressive of a typical emphasis on the obedience characteristic of the sacraments. Obedience is seen here not so much as the response to demands or commandments but more as adherence to basic principles or "natural" laws of God's created order.

Eighth, the sacraments use common things to symbolize intangible reality. A sacrament is defined in the Anglican catechism as "an outward and visible sign of an inward and spiritual grace." Any attempt to explain or express divine action or presence in human terms must of necessity use symbolic forms and actions. The hands symbolize the power of God. Water symbolizes

15

cleansing. Bread and wine symbolize Christ's body and blood. The symbols used in the sacraments make it possible for the church to experience the presence of Christ and witness God at work among people. The use of common symbols repeatedly throughout the ages unites the church across time and sect and expresses its faithfulness to its one Lord.

Ninth, the sacraments are acts of the corporate body. When one individual is blessed, baptized, or confirmed, the whole body of the church participates in the sacrament. Viewing a sacrament as involving only a single individual and God ignores the basic context in which the sacraments are celebrated. Without the church there are no sacraments. The celebration of most sacraments in a congregational worship setting demonstrates their essentially corporate nature. The church is the covenant community. As such, it participates fully in the sacraments in which persons make individual covenants with God. The expression of an individual affects the entire community. In baptism, for example, the family of God receives a new member who contributes to the family and also looks to it for strength and support.

Tenth, the sacraments serve as avenues to new life. Through Jesus Christ, God offers newness of life. Freedom replaces bondage and hope takes the place of despair. Participation in the sacraments of the church makes it possible for individuals to enjoy the kind of covenant relationship with others and with God that characterizes the new life. The sacraments offer unique opportunities for communion with the living Christ. Such fellowship serves as the backbone for the new life God gives us, which we are challenged to accept and share with others.

Eleventh, the sacraments are ritual acts with specified procedures. The church's practice of the sacraments is based on its best understanding of the intent and nature of each sacrament. In many churches sacramental procedures are based on centuries of tradition. Yet procedures do sometimes change over time, usually for identifiable reasons. When they do change it is usually not without major institutional struggles and adjustments. In the RLDS tradition sacramental procedures are, for the most part, carefully specified. All sacraments are to be performed only by priesthood members holding certain offices. The form and sometimes also the words are specified. The recipients of some of the sacraments must meet certain qualifications.

Standardized sacramental procedures are in some cases marks of identity of a particular denomination (e.g., baptism at the age of eight). In other cases standardized procedures are marks of unity throughout Christianity (e.g., the use of bread and wine for the Lord's Supper).

Sacraments in the Life of the Church

Historically the sacraments have been held in high esteem by Reorganized Latter Day Saints. Celebration of these rites has been a focal point of the church's gathering together for corporate worship. Yet the church is called to be God's agent of redemption to the world. As such, the church receives and uses the sacraments not for its own benefit but for the benefit of the world it serves. The God who acts and the Christ who is present in the sacraments sustain the church and its members so they in turn can reach out to others. Jesus used his association with God and the strength derived therefrom as sustenance for his life, which he sacrificed so humanity could be saved. Likewise, the church uses the sacraments as a major form of sustenance for the sacrificial life it is called to live in the world.

Baptism, the Lord's Supper, confirmation, the blessing of children, ordination, and marriage are normally celebrated in a public worship setting. This is appropriate to the corporate nature of the sacraments. Private celebration of these sacraments is discouraged as a general rule but sometimes occurs when circumstances make a public worship setting impractical.

Specific procedures for the sacraments themselves are set down in church law. These are described in subsequent chapters of this book. However, the general worship setting in which each sacrament is celebrated can vary widely. Regardless of how the service of worship is arranged, several ingredients are important and usually find expression when the sacraments are celebrated.

First is the expression of praise and thanksgiving. When we gather together for worship, we turn toward the God who created and sustains us. God is the giver of life, of the Son, and of the sacraments, and it is God who calls the church to mission. Recognition of all that God has done for humanity issues forth in expressions of praise and thanksgiving, which are the beginning points of Christian worship.

Second is the acknowledgment of human dependency on God. In the face of God's greatness we sense our unworthiness and need to repent and be forgiven. We confess that we are sinners and live in separation from God. Our shortcomings and weaknesses are exposed as we lay ourselves bare at the mercy of a loving God. Repentance and confession are received by God with love, forgiveness, and acceptance. This mood is one of preparation. We wait and prepare to receive what God offers us. Contemplation and meditation occur through self-examination.

Third is our preparation for receiving God through the sacraments. Here we contemplate the meaning and importance of the ritual act itself. The scriptural testimony is shared and interpreted so both candidate and congregation are reminded of what they are about to receive and do. Here is proclaimed God's all-encompassing forgiveness through which our sin is absolved.

Fourth, the sacrament is celebrated. God gives and we receive. Through the presence of Christ God moves again to bring about the divine purpose of the world's redemption. Through symbolic act the mysterious God is made real to finite beings. Our response is that of glad acceptance. We receive our God and submit ourselves to all that is required of us.

Fifth is our response to God's action in the sacrament. We offer our lives in service to God and dedicate all that we are and have. We reaffirm our desire and willingness to participate fully in the divine mission to which we have been called. Knowing that God is with us, we move out from the worship experience strengthened, inspired, and challenged.

The worship setting is important to the sacraments. In worship we prepare for, receive, and respond to God's action present in the sacraments. Planning and preparing for sacramental worship is an important task to be undertaken deliberately and with care. The way in which we approach this task reveals or betrays how important we think the sacraments are to us and to the church.

Activities and Discussion Questions

1. Look up the word *sacrament* in various dictionaries and encyclopedias. Then write out your own definition. Share your discoveries and your own definition with others in a group. Or discuss the first three paragraphs of this chapter as an entire class.

2. Go to a college or public library and do some research to find out which rites are regarded as sacraments in the various Christian denominations. What is significant about the results you find?

3. Invite a Roman Catholic priest to talk to your group about the meaning and role of sacraments in his church. Or interview a priest for the same purpose. Ministers of other denominations could also be contacted.

4. Review the eleven characteristics of sacraments described on pages 12–17. Which do you think are most important? Why? Which ones do you think are unimportant or invalid? Why? What other characteristics would you add?

5. Some of the characteristics on pages 12–17 emphasize God's action in the sacraments; others emphasize human action. In your own view, which of these do you personally emphasize? Which do you think most Reorganized Latter Day Saints emphasize? Are you satisfied with what you understand is the present emphasis? Why or why not?

6. How important are the sacraments (a) to you as an individual, (b) to your local congregation, and (c) to the church at large? Illustrate your answers by reference to how the sacraments are practiced in the church.

7. Write a letter to a hypothetical non-RLDS friend explaining what you believe to be the RLDS understanding of the sacraments. Compare your letter with those written by others in a group. Can the differences be reconciled? How much variation of views with regard to the sacraments should be permitted in the church?
8. What do you understand to be the mission of the church? What has God called the church to do? How do the sacraments fit into this mission and calling?
9. What do the sacraments do for people that they cannot receive some other way?
10. Review the five ingredients of the worship setting for sacraments found on pages 18-19. Which of these is more important? Why? Are any dispensable? Why? Should others be included also? Why?
11. Secure a copy of *Exploring the Faith* (Herald House, 1987). Read pages 216-224. What additional help does this provide for understanding the sacraments of the church?

Notes

1. Luke 22:19 and I Corinthians 11:24.

CHAPTER 2

Baptism

Meanings of Baptism

Baptism in the RLDS Church has many meanings. Some of the most important are the following:

- entrance into church membership
- remission of sin
- an act of repentance
- commitment to Christ
- covenant with God
- expression of faith and trust
- gateway to salvation
- demonstration of God's love
- new birth and new life
- obedience to God's command
- recognition of accountability

Following is a brief explanation of each of these meanings.

Entrance into Church Membership

For Reorganized Latter Day Saints baptism is seen as the first in a two-part rite, or process, of initiation into the church. The second part of the process is confirmation, which will be discussed in the next chapter.[1] The initiatory role of baptism emphasizes the voluntary decision of the individual to join the church. The baptized member's name is entered in the church records both at Headquarters and in the local congregation. But joining the church, like joining any organization, involves more than this. It involves association and involvement in a community of people united in purpose. Baptism makes one a *participant* in the life and work of the church and therefore a co-worker with God.

Baptism represents entrance into the particular denomination with which one affiliates. For us this means that we are baptized into the Reorganized Church of Jesus Christ of Latter Day Saints and become members of that particular fellowship. Baptism also signifies commitment to the universal task of Christianity to which the contributions of other Christians are acknowledged and appreciated. In the Book of Mormon we read that "they who were baptized in the name of Jesus were called the church of Christ."[2] Further, Paul says, "By one Spirit are we all baptized into one body.... Ye are the body of Christ, and members in particular."[3]

Remission of Sin

One principal result or effect of baptism is the remission of sin. Many references from the church's three books of scripture support this understanding of baptism. See for example the Bible, Mark 1:3 (1:4 IV), Acts 2:38 and 22:16, Matthew 5:4; Doctrine and Covenants

32:2g, 49:2g, and 18:4d; and the Book of Mormon, Alma 5:25 and III Nephi 14:3.

The idea of remission of sin can have a number of interpretations. It can mean that God forgives sin and thereby restores the divine/human relationship. It can mean that a debt is canceled—that God does not require us to "pay" for our wrongdoing but instead eliminates its effect on us and our relationships to God and others. It also refers to the washing away of sin as symbolized by the cleansing effect of immersion in water.

However understood, the remission of sin refers to the action of God in the context of the human condition. God is the only one who can forgive us, thereby bridging the gap that separates humanity from divinity. We cannot do this ourselves. In the words of Paul, "All have sinned, and come short of the glory of God."[4] Everyone, then, is in need of forgiveness.

As far as what actually happens in baptism is concerned two views are possible. One view is that the candidate's sin is taken away at the moment of baptism. The other view is that baptism is the symbol for and celebration of the forgiveness of God, which is an ever-present reality in our lives before, at, and after the actual baptismal experience. Both views emphasize the action of God in human lives and find expression in people's beliefs.

An Act of Repentance

An important reference in the Doctrine and Covenants related to baptism and repentance reads as follows:

And again by way of commandment to the church concerning the manner of baptism:

25

> All those who humble themselves before God and desire to be baptized, and come forth with broken hearts and contrite spirits, and witness before the church that they have truly repented of all their sins, and are willing to take upon them the name of Jesus Christ, having a determination to serve him to the end, and truly manifest by their works that they have received of the Spirit of Christ unto the remission of their sins, shall be received by baptism into his church.[5]

One of the important reasons for making the decision to be baptized is one's need for and feeling of repentance. This is likely to play a greater part in the decision of an adult than that of a child who has just reached the age of eight. As demonstrated in the scripture just quoted, repentance is related to one's behavior as well as attitude. A person who has repented will behave differently as well as think and feel differently.

Viewing baptism as the event that changes a person from sinner to nonsinner has serious limitations. Both baptized and unbaptized persons live continually in the context and condition of sin and therefore constantly need to live in an attitude of repentance. Our view of baptism as an act of repentance must allow for this reality. There *is* a sense in which repentance comes before and is in fact a prerequisite for baptism. Repentance also, however, follows baptism.

It should be noted that Doctrine and Covenants 17:7a-d is not used as a legal prerequisite for baptism. Whether candidates "have truly repented of all their sins" is impossible to determine in any measurable sense. Any attempt to deny baptism to certain individuals because of particular "sins" of which they may or may not have repented would raise difficult theological and administrative questions.

The role of repentance in baptism is abundantly documented in scripture. See for example in the Bible, Matthew 3:11 (3:38 IV), Mark 1:4 (1:3 IV); Doctrine and Covenants 16:4e, 16:6d, 18:4d, 32:2g, 39:2b, 42:2d, 49:2g, 55:lc, 83:4c, 104:10; and Book of Mormon, Alma 5:25, 7:41; Moroni 6:2, and III Nephi 12:29. Repentance is the way we open our lives to receive that which God does for us.

Commitment to Christ

When I was baptized, the officiating minister entered the water, turned to me, and said, "Do you promise to follow Jesus Christ for the rest of your life?" I replied, "Yes, I do." I was subsequently baptized and have never forgotten the promise that I made at that time.

When Jesus called disciples he issued them an invitation. He called them to follow him and to assist him in that great work which God had sent him to do. Likewise he calls us. The scriptures say, "All are called."[6] Baptism represents the individual's affirmative response to the greatest call that can ever come to a human being. In Moroni 6:3 we read, "And none were received unto baptism save they took upon them the name of Christ, having a determination to serve him to the end."

The decision to follow Christ carries with it a commitment to be involved in the task and ministry to which our Lord himself was dedicated. Christ is both example and leader. The way he responded to life situations serves as a model for us as we are confronted by the challenge of ministry in today's world. Christ is our leader in that he continues to call us day after day to follow him.

The relationship of baptism to the Christ is further expressed in the concept of being baptized *in Christ's name*. We are baptized into Christ and carry his name with us by calling ourselves "Christians." We "take upon ourselves" Christ's name and are expected to carry it with honor, humility, and integrity.

Covenant with God

Baptism is a covenant entered into between the individual and God. This is more than the expression of commitment to Christ mentioned in the previous paragraph. It is a two-way relationship that individualizes and extends God's covenant with the chosen people expressed in the words, "I will walk among you, and will be your God, and ye shall be my people."[7] In the concept of covenant, divine/human action and intent come together. The overemphasis of either at the expense of the other results in distortion.

It is appropriate, however, to see God as the initiator of the covenant and ourselves as respondents. In the covenant God offers Godself to us as creator, sustainer, protector, redeemer, and judge. Our response is one of acceptance of the covenant and commitment to its demands. In baptism individuals accept God's claim on their lives and covenant to be God's people. We respond to Alma's admonition, "Enter into a covenant with [God] to keep his commandments, and witness it to him this day by going into the waters of baptism."[8]

Expression of Faith and Trust

Baptism is an expression of our faith and trust in God. We place our lives in God's hands and pledge to follow wherever we are led. A Christian life is characterized by risk and uncertainty. We do not know *where* we are going or *what* will happen to us. Yet we do know *who* we are following. Our faith is in God to whom we owe our lives.

Placing our bodies in the hands of the minister symbolizes our faith and trust in God. We express confidence in those who have been called by God and recognized by the congregation to perform this sacrament on their behalf.

In addition to faith in God in a general sense, baptism is also an expression of faith that God will live up to the covenant promise to walk among us and be our God and to extend to us forgiveness for our sin. Alma admonishes, "Come and be baptized... that you may have faith on the Lamb of God, who takes away the sins of the world."[9]

Gateway to Salvation

There are various ideas about the meaning of salvation among Reorganized Latter Day Saints. Some interpret it in otherworldly terms with emphasis on the place to which one goes after death. Others view it as freedom from sin in this world.

However understood, the scriptures make it quite clear that salvation is one of the rewards or benefits coming to those who are baptized. In Doctrine and Covenants 68:1g we read, "He that believeth, and is baptized, shall be saved." Words to the same effect appear in other places in the scriptures also.[10] The relationship between salvation and baptism is recognized by many denominations. Their position, generally, is that baptism into any Christian body is valid in terms of its saving effect. Reorganized Latter Day Saints, however, have traditionally maintained that baptism by our own authorized ministers into our own church is the only legitimate form of baptism. The church does not accept people into membership based on previous baptisms in other churches. However, to claim that people baptized into other churches are not eligible for salvation is to deny God the freedom to work through whomever God chooses. Such a position is difficult to justify and is no longer the prevailing view among RLDS members.

However we might understand the relationship between baptism and salvation, the important thing is that baptism is as central to the church today as it was in the 1830s or at any time in the entire history of Christianity. We affirm that it is a sacrament that God has placed in the church for the benefit of humankind. Whether or not submission to the rite of baptism in a particular church, or in any church, is necessary for salvation or whether being baptized guarantees a person salvation are questions that God alone can answer. We should remember that salvation is God's gift to us, and this is symbolized by the sacrament of baptism.

The inadequacy of simplistic answers is further pointed out if we look at II Nephi 13:24-30. Here baptism is seen to be the beginning of a lifelong relationship rather than the guarantee of a particular place or result. Verse 29 says, "Wherefore, you must press forward with a steadfastness in Christ, having a perfect brightness of hope, and a love of God and of all [people]." One's whole life response is just as important as beginning at the right place. In this context we understand what it means to "endure to the end."[11]

Demonstration of God's Love

God loves and cares for all creation. This is a central affirmation of Christianity in general and of the RLDS faith in particular. Every person has worth in the sight of God, not because people are deserving but because God is loving. Baptism is a special, personal expression of God's concern for the individual. Baptism demonstrates universals in a particular way that transforms general principles into experienced realities. It changes "God loves all people" to "God loves me."

God's love for people is most concretely expressed in baptism through the witnessing and participating congregation. The welcome extended by the congregation to the newly baptized member expresses, by the warmth of human relationship, God's love for that person.

New Birth and New Life

In the fourth Gospel Jesus says to Nicodemus, "No one can enter the kingdom of God without being born of water and Spirit."[12] Jesus was, of course, referring to baptism as the process by which we participate with him in the crucial realities of death and resurrection. Going down into the water symbolizes crucifixion and burial. Emerging from the water symbolizes resurrection and the rising to a new life. Paul expressed it like this: "Therefore we are buried with him by baptism into death; that like as Christ was raised up from the dead by the glory of the Father, even so we also should walk in newness of life."[13]

Being born again gives us new life. This life is different from the old. This does not mean that we have abandoned sin altogether. Our experience tells us that we have not. Instead, new life brings us freedom from the guilt, meaninglessness, and despair that characterize our old lives. We now live with the knowledge that we are loved and accepted despite our sinful condition. New life brings with it acceptance of self and others, meaningful participation in contemporary life, and hope for the future which is in God's hands.

In baptism God claims individuals and recreates them through rebirth into new life. This life is God's gift made possible through the life and ministry of Jesus Christ. In baptism we are changed and remade by God.

Obedience to God's Command

Baptism is both sacrament (act of God) and ordinance (command of God). The human action in baptism is response to the command of God. Jesus recognized baptism as the will of God. He responded to John's reluctance to baptize him by saying, "It becometh us to fulfill all righteousness."[14] In II Nephi we find an additional explanation of Jesus' baptism: "He [Jesus] would be obedient to him [God] in keeping his commandments."[15] Jesus is described in the Book of Mormon as saying, "Ye must repent, and become as a little child, and be baptized in my name."[16] The Doctrine and Covenants also expresses baptism as a commandment in several places.[17]

The natural response of the person who wishes to follow Christ is to do God's will. Obedience to the commands of God is an important way of expressing one's commitment to Christ.

Recognition of Accountability

The term "age of accountability" means more than a minimum age for baptism. It also suggests that we are accountable to God for our decisions, our resources, our whole lives. In baptism we recognize that we are partners with God in the exercise of wise stewardship over all that is in our possession. We answer to God for what has been entrusted to our care. We have dared to take upon ourselves the name of Christ. Something is expected of us.

Not only are we accountable to God but we must also answer to our fellow Christians. The baptismal occasion is public in nature. We accept God's claim on our lives in the presence of members of the community that we join. Members of the congregation are accountable to each other for their Christian discipleship.

We are also accountable to the world for our identity as Christians. In baptism we take on the responsibility of assisting God in the redemption of the world.

Baptismal Procedures

From the earliest days of the Latter Day Saint movement baptism has been administered according to the procedure specified in the Doctrine and Covenants as follows:

> The person who is called of God and has authority from Jesus Christ to baptize, shall go down into the water with the person who has presented him or herself for baptism, and shall say, calling him or her by name:
>
> Having been commissioned of Jesus Christ, I baptize you in the name of the Father, and of the Son, and of the Holy Ghost, Amen.
>
> Then shall he immerse him or her in the water, and come forth again out of the water. [18]

The earliest published form of this instruction includes different wording for the baptismal formula. It says, "Having authority given me of Jesus Christ, I baptize you in the name of the Father, and of the Son, and of the Holy Ghost, Amen." [19] This was replaced by the current wording in two published versions of the "Articles and Covenants of the Church of Christ" in 1835. [20] The earlier wording has been preserved, however, in the Book of Mormon down to the present time."[21] The practice is for officiants to use their choice of these two wordings when administering baptism.

The General Conference of the church did go on record in 1862, however, favoring the use of the Doctrine and Covenants version containing the word "commissioned." At the same time the Conference recognized the words "authority" and "commission" as being synonymous.[22] This distinction, however, is omitted from recent publications of this resolution. The resolution now reads, "That whoever administers the ordinance of baptism should use the precise words given in the law of the Book of Covenants, and not substitute his own words in place of the words of God."[23]

Faithful adherence to the specific words makes baptism one of the few occasions on which prescribed statements or prayers are used in the RLDS Church. The other occasions are the Lord's Supper and the marriage ceremony.

There is no deviation from the practice of immersion. All three books of scripture are used as the basis for this practice.[24]

Section 17 of the Doctrine and Covenants specifies that priests and elders are the only priesthood offices authorized by the church to perform baptisms.[25] The term *elder* is construed to mean all people ordained to the Melchisedec priesthood.

The RLDS Church requires that persons reach the "age of accountability" before being baptized. This is specified in the Book of Mormon[26] and Doctrine and Covenants.[27] Both of these references date back before the organization of the church. The "age of accountability" became identified as eight years at least as early as spring 1831. This is the time at which Joseph Smith dictated his revision of Genesis 17:7 which reads as follows:

> And I will establish a covenant of circumscision with thee, and it shall be my covenant between me and thee, and thy seed after thee, in their generations; that thou mayest know forever that children are not accountable before me until they are eight years old.[28]

Although the verse in question does not mention baptism specifically, the connection is clear. The age requirement for baptism is reaffirmed in a document dated November 1831 dictated by Joseph Smith. This time the reference to baptism is explicit: "Children shall be baptized for the remission of their sins when eight years old."[29] The age requirement was reaffirmed by the 1904 General Conference with the words "children under eight years of age are not eligible for baptism in the church."[30] This rule is still in effect and is rigidly enforced.[31]

Planning the Service of Baptism

The following suggestions are offered for consideration by those who plan baptismal services:

1. Baptism is a special occasion for the candidate and for the church. The importance of baptism is symbolized by holding the baptismal service at a time and place at which all regular attenders in the congregation can be present. Scheduling baptisms at the regular worship hour on Sunday is preferable to holding them at a time or place when few people will be present. The congregation's presence offers support to the candidate and also expresses the corporate nature of baptism.

2. The congregation that has several candidates ready for baptism at about the same time may wish to schedule a baptismal service for a special day. If the

candidates are children, Children's Day may be chosen for this purpose. In the early Christian Church baptisms were almost always held at Easter following extensive preparation for the candidates. Baptism at Easter symbolically relates Jesus' new life of resurrection and the candidate's new life in baptism and church membership. Congregations may wish to adopt this tradition using the season of Lent (forty days plus six Sundays before Easter) as a period of preparation for the candidates and also for the congregation.

3. It is often practical to hold more than one baptism in a single service of worship. This practice is appropriate, if it is not abused. When baptizing large numbers of candidates in the same service, care should be taken to avoid a "production line" effect. The baptism of each individual is important to the candidate and congregation. This can be recognized with careful planning and coordination. On occasion it may be found more appropriate to hold two baptismal services than to include too many candidates in one service.

4. Baptismal services usually include a statement addressed to the candidate(s). This is often referred to as "the charge." Such remarks can include comments on the significance of the decision being made by the candidate and also on the privileges and responsibilities of church membership. Another important element to include is assurance of the love and presence of God in the lives of people. Baptism is the response of individuals to the initiative of God in their lives. This needs to be recognized verbally in the service. The spoken word should not be addressed exclusively to the candidate(s). An important function of baptism is the recalling and reliving of the baptismal experience by all who have been baptized previously. The words to the candidate

and to the congregation may be combined into one statement or may be separated. These statements should be long enough to significantly address the occasion but not too long to become tedious. Whether there are one or two statements, a total length of ten minutes is usually sufficient. The remarks should be to the point and based on appropriate scriptures such as those mentioned earlier in this chapter.

5. The candidate's response is symbolized by the act of going down into the water and submitting to the baptismal rite. Response to God's call to baptism could also be expressed in a brief personal statement from the candidate. This statement would include a brief expression of thanksgiving to God and the church and an indication of commitment to Christ. This is most appropriately done after the charge and before the baptism but could follow the baptism. An alternative procedure would be for the candidate to give affirmative response to a question such as, "Do you accept God's call to service and dedicate your life to following Christ?" asked by a minister or member of the congregation.

6. The congregation's response can be symbolized in several ways. One or two representatives from the congregation could affirm support for the newly baptized member and express their commitment to Christ. The congregation's response to the act of baptism could be expressed through a unison prayer or carefully selected prayer, hymn, or other statement. Response by the congregation is appropriate in light of the corporate nature of baptism and may be offered in response to statements addressed to the congregation in the spoken word.

7. Where several people are being baptized in the same service, it is customary for the congregation to

sing one stanza of a hymn between each baptism to allow time for one candidate to leave the water and another to enter. The stanzas need to be chosen in such a way that the words are generally appropriate to the occasion. Hymns 350-357 in *Hymns of the Saints* (Herald Publishing House, 1981) specifically relate to baptism. As an alternative to hymns at this point in the service, an appropriate instrumental or vocal solo or scripture readings could be used.

8. When the newly baptized persons are away from the sanctuary changing their clothes, the rest of the congregation continues in worship. Carefully selected hymns and scriptures are appropriate at this point in the service.

9. After the candidates have returned, a brief pastoral statement of commission is appropriate. This should include recognition of the significance of what has occurred in the service and an invitation to the entire congregation to move from the occasion in a spirit of dedication and commitment. Toward the end of the service a statement welcoming the newly baptized individual into church membership is sometimes included. Whether this is more appropriate in the baptismal service or in the confirmation service is subject to interpretation. Although these two sacraments are not normally performed in the same service of worship they are closely related. If church membership is seen as being conferred only after confirmation, then a statement of welcome more properly belongs in the confirmation service. However, if a person is considered a member of the church after having been baptized then such a statement properly belongs in the baptismal service.

10. Where only one or two candidates are being baptized, there may be opportunities for other acts of worship addressed specifically to the candidates themselves. One possibility is a brief statement by a member of the candidate's family or one from the congregation who has known the candidate a long time. This statement could reflect on the candidate's life and the events that have brought him or her to baptism. When a child is being baptized, the showing of several slides depicting the child's growth and development might be particularly appropriate. Another option is for the congregation to make an appropriate poster or banner celebrating the occasion. The finished product could be presented to the candidate toward the end of the service. The signature of each member of the congregation in attendance might appear somewhere on the presentation piece.

The candidate may be invited to share with the congregation an especially meaningful story, scripture, hymn, or recorded song. Or the candidate could be invited to read the scriptural account of Jesus' baptism by John at an appropriate time in the service.

Activities and Discussion Questions

1. Which of the eleven meanings of baptism described in this chapter have particular appeal to you? Why? Which have no appeal to you at all? Why? What meanings other than those mentioned can you think of?

2. Attend a baptismal service of another faith. What differences do you perceive? What did you like about the service? What did you not like? Did you experience anything that could enhance RLDS baptismal services if used?

3. Is the insistence on total immersion as the only valid means of baptism necessary in your opinion? What are grounds for arguing that it is or that it is not? Compare the symbolism of pouring, sprinkling, and immersion.

4. What *really happens* to the candidate at the time of baptism? How is the candidate different after baptism?

5. What are the prerequisites for a person to be baptized? Be specific. What are some of the problems of interpreting Doctrine and Covenants 17:7 in this regard? What kind of case can be made for having no prerequisites at all for baptism?

6. Write a one-sentence definition of baptism. Discuss it with others in a group.

7. What essential differences in meaning exist between RLDS baptism and infant baptism as practiced by other faiths? Invite a minister from another faith into your group to talk about the meaning of baptism.

8. Using concordances to the three books of scripture, look up all the references to baptism that you can find. What important concepts do you discover?

9. Suggest some ways that baptismal services can be made more significant to the candidate and congregation.

10. Why is it important that baptism be celebrated in a public worship setting rather than in a private ceremony?

11. What do you believe about the state of children under eight years of age? Do you think that the minimum age for baptism is appropriate? Why or why not?

12. Discuss the pros and cons of the assertion that baptism is essential for salvation. What is salvation? Does baptism guarantee salvation?
13. Is baptism primarily a divine act or a human act?
14. Do some research into early Christian baptismal practice. What understandings are gained? What meanings were present? Who officiated in baptism? When and where did baptisms occur? What procedures were used?
15. What are the reasons for requiring that people be rebaptized to join the RLDS Church if they have already been baptized in another Christian denomination? What points, if any, could be made in favor of allowing people to join the church without rebaptism?

Notes

1. It is possible to perceive entrance into the church as a three-part rite if the blessing of a child is regarded as the first part.
2. III Nephi 12:13.
3. I Corinthians 12:13, 27.
4. Romans 3:23.
5. Doctrine and Covenants 17:7.
6. Doctrine and Covenants 119:8b and 156:9b.
7. Leviticus 26:12.
8. Alma 5:27.
9. Alma 5:25.
10. See in the Bible, Mark 16:16 (16:15 IV), Acts 16:31, and I Peter 3:21; Doctrine and Covenants 16:4e, 17:5d, and 105:11c; Book of Mormon, II Nephi 6:48.
11. Doctrine and Covenants 16:4e and 17:5d.
12. John 3:5 NRSV.
13. Romans 6:4.
14. Matthew 3:15 KJV (3:43 IV).
15. II Nephi 13:9.
16. III Nephi 5:39.
17. Doctrine and Covenants 16:6d, 32:2g, and 68:4a-b.

18. Doctrine and Covenants 17:21b-d.
19. *The Evening and the Morning Star* I, no. 1 (June 1832): 1. See also II, no. 13 (June 1833): 1; and *Book of Commandments* (1833), chapter 24, paragraph 53.
20. *The Evening and the Morning Star* I, no. 1, reprinted with alterations in January 1835, and the first edition of the Doctrine and Covenants published in August 1835.
21. III Nephi 5:25.
22. *Saints' Herald* 3, no. 5 (November 1862): 117.
23. *Rules and Resolutions,* 1990 Edition (Herald Publishing House, 1990), GCR 48, adopted October 7, 1862.
24. See for example in the Bible, Matthew 3:16 (3:45 IV), Mark 1:9-10 (1:7-8 IV), Romans 6:4-5, Colossians 2:12; Doctrine and Covenants 17:21; and Book of Mormon, III Nephi 5:24-26.
25. Doctrine and Covenants 17:8b, d, and 10a.
26. Moroni 8:11.
27. Doctrine and Covenants 16:6d.
28. Genesis 17:11 IV.
29. Doctrine and Covenants 68:4b.
30. *Rules and Resolutions,* 1990 Edition (Herald Publishing House, 1990), GCR 552, adopted April 15, 1904.
31. See official statement by the First Presidency in the *Saints Herald* 123, no. 11 (November 1976): 4.

CHAPTER 3

Confirmation

Confirmation, otherwise known as baptism of the Spirit, follows baptism by water and completes a person's initiation into the church. The only prerequisite for the rite of confirmation is that a person be baptized into the RLDS Church.

Confirmation sometimes occurs immediately following baptism in the same service of worship. More usually, however, several days or weeks elapse between baptism and confirmation. Allowing a lengthy period to pass between the two is discouraged. The two rites are seen as distinct but related.

The *Church Administrator's Handbook* speaks to this matter of timing:

> The sacraments of baptism and confirmation usually require separate services for full impact in the lives of candidates. Such separation permits more adequate attention to these distinctive worship experiences. Separation provides time for encouraging and instructing new members (Doctrine and Covenants 17:18). It also

provides opportunity for each person to prepare adequately for the importance of the confirmation service.

Nevertheless, these two phases of the new birth, baptism and confirmation, belong together. Their unity will suffer from any considerable separation, because they are intended to support and dignify each other. Therefore, the time lapse between baptism and confirmation should not be too long.[1]

One purpose of waiting awhile before confirmation is that instruction in the duties and privileges of membership may be received by the newly baptized person. This requirement is specified in Doctrine and Covenants 17:18b. Present-day practice usually provides for such instruction to be received before baptism itself. This was probably not done in the early days of the church but was sometimes attended to between baptism and confirmation. The counsel referred to in Section 17 was not always adhered to in the early church. In Section 52, several traveling missionaries were admonished to "preach by the way in every congregation, baptizing by water, and the laying on of the hands by the water's side."[2] The length of time elapsing between baptism and confirmation was, and still is, to a large degree dictated by circumstances. Where the candidate is baptized and will not have access to elders of the church for confirmation in the near future, the confirmation is performed right away. In situations where such access is anticipated it is more likely for some time to elapse between the two sacraments.

Confirmation is administered by the laying on of hands. The candidate sits in a chair and two[3] elders[4] lay their hands on the candidate's head, one offering the prayer of confirmation. There are no prescribed words that must be included in the prayer of confirmation.

44

The practice of confirmation has broad scriptural support,[5] as has the specific method of using the laying on of hands.[6] However, the concept of "laying on of hands," as it is used to refer to confirmation, is entirely absent from the Book of Mormon. It is also interesting to note that there are no Conference resolutions on the books speaking to the matter of confirmation.

Meanings of Confirmation

Confirmation has two important meanings in the RLDS Church. These are entrance into full membership and reception of the Holy Spirit.

Entrance into full membership

Confirmation is the second part of the two-part process of initiation into the church. Whereas the emphasis in baptism tends to be on the candidate's decision to request baptism, the emphasis in confirmation is on the church's acceptance of the person into full membership. The confirmed person is granted specific rights and responsibilities of membership "in good standing" including voting in church business meetings and partaking of the Lord's Supper.[7] As mentioned earlier, by the time of confirmation the candidate has taken a course of prebaptismal instruction relating to church belief, practice, and the responsibilities of membership.

The prayer of confirmation will usually include direct reference to the candidate being granted membership in the church. A phrase such as "We confirm you a member of the Reorganized Church of Jesus Christ of Latter Day Saints" may be used but is not mandatory. The prayer also petitions God to grant the candidate strength to responsibly live out the duties of member-ship.

Following confirmation, the person's name is entered in local and World Church records as being a member of the Reorganized Church of Jesus Christ of Latter Day Saints and of the local branch or congregation in particular.

The role of the congregation in confirmation is important. The community of members recognizes the decision and commitment made by the candidate in baptism and welcomes the person into the fellowship of the church.

Reception of the Holy Spirit

The scriptures contain abundant references to the Holy Spirit's indwelling following baptism.[8] Specifically, this concept is based on the biblical records of the Spirit descending on Jesus following his baptism by John.[9] In confirmation God grants the Holy Spirit to lead, guide, and comfort the person who has made the commitment to follow Christ in baptism. The action of God in the life of the individual is sometimes dramatically demonstrated by the use of such words as "Receive ye the gift of the Holy Spirit (or Ghost)" in the confirmation prayer.

It is unusual, however, to find a total denial of the Spirit's presence before baptism or confirmation. The usual view is that the Spirit (the "spark of divinity" or "the true light, which enlightens everyone"[10]) is present in all people but that confirmation brings a fuller measure of the Spirit into a person's life. A person's commitment to Christian discipleship brings a greater awareness and sensitivity to the Holy Spirit.

Numerous images of the nature of the Spirit are evident in RLDS literature. Images prevalent in connection with confirmation are guide, comforter, giver of strength, protector, teacher, and companion. Emphasis is on the Spirit's power to help the person keep the covenant made in baptism. Although the baptism of water is usually regarded as the symbol for cleansing and remission of sin, the symbolism of fire associated with the Spirit can also have this same meaning. In the Book of Mormon we read, "After they had been received in baptism, and were wrought upon and cleansed by the power of the Holy Ghost, they were numbered among the people of the church of Christ."[11] In the Doctrine and Covenants we read of "remission of sins by baptism and by fire; yea, even the Holy Ghost."[12]

An examination of the various references in the three books of scripture to the Holy Spirit's presence after baptism reveals several possible approaches to the Spirit's bestowal. Although confirmation by the rite of the laying on of hands has probably been practiced since the beginning of the RLDS Church, not all scriptures specify this procedure.

As mentioned earlier, the Book of Mormon contains no references to this rite but rather contains such references as "as many as were baptized in the name of Jesus were filled with the Holy Ghost."[13] This could be interpreted in a way that suggests that a rite of confirmation is not necessary but that the Holy Spirit's presence is a "normal" result of baptism in the fashion recorded of Jesus in the Bible.[14] That procedures for the rite of confirmation may have taken awhile to be worked out is indicated by a comparison of the earliest (1830-1832) and later (1835) versions of Doctrine and Covenants 17:8b-e. In reference to the duties of the elder this passage reads:

Early Version	Late Version
(*Book of Commandments*, chapter 24, paragraphs 32, 33, and 34)	(Doctrine and Covenants, Section 17:8b-e)
32. An apostle is an elder, and it is his calling to baptize and to ordain other elders, priests, teachers and deacons, and to administer the flesh and blood of Christ	b. An apostle is an elder, and it is his calling to baptize, and to ordain other elders, priests, teachers, and deacons, and to administer bread and wine—the emblems of the flesh and blood of Christ—
	c. and to confirm those who are baptized into the church, by the laying on of hands for the baptism of fire and the Holy Ghost, according to the Scriptures;
according to the scriptures; 33. And to teach, expound, exhort, baptize, and watch over the church;	d. and to teach, expound, exhort, baptize, and watch over the church;
34. And to confirm the church by the laying on of the hands, and the giving of the Holy Ghost.	e. and to confirm the church by the laying on of the hands, and the giving of the Holy Ghost.

It is possible that the addition of paragraph c above in the later text was to clarify procedures which in paragraph e are quite vague. However, considering the biblical evidences[15] of the use of the rite in the early New Testament Church, it would be premature to conclude that the rite did not exist from the beginning of the Latter Day Saint movement.

Planning the Confirmation Service

The following suggestions may be helpful to those who are planning confirmation services.

1. Plan the entire service of worship to focus on the sacrament of confirmation. Adding confirmations at the last minute to an already planned preaching or Communion service usually results in an overcrowded service and demeaning of the sacrament.

2. Confirmation is important in the life of the church. It is appropriately planned for the main Sunday service or some other time when a majority of the congregation can be present. Confirmation services held at odd hours or in unusual places tend to draw only a few people and therefore lack the corporate element important to most sacraments.

3. As with baptism, care should be taken to avoid a "production line" effect when large numbers of candidates are confirmed in any one service.

4. Individuals are sometimes baptized and confirmed at the same service of worship. This is particularly advisable if the candidate will not have the opportunity for fellowship in a congregation for some time after baptism and would therefore need to wait months or years before being confirmed. However, celebrating the two sacraments in the same service may obscure the distinction between them. On the other hand, it is inadvisable for too long a period of time to transpire between a person's baptism and confirmation. A separation of more than a few weeks runs the risk of ignoring the close connection between the two. A space of one to three weeks is in most cases appropriate.

5. The confirmation itself is usually preceded in the service by a statement explaining the meaning of the sacrament. Such a statement is appropriately ad-

dressed to the candidate but is also directed to the congregation. This statement is normally made by a minister from the rostrum. One or more members of the congregation might also share in the spoken word. Whatever the form, this statement needs to be fairly brief (not exceeding ten to fifteen minutes) and focused on the significance of confirmation and membership in the church.

6. A statement of welcome into membership or presentation of the candidate is appropriate following the confirmation if this was not included in the baptismal service. The congregation may wish to present the new member with a copy of *Church Members Manual*, a New Testament, Bible, Book of Mormon, Doctrine and Covenants, or other appropriate book or gift. Such a gift symbolizes the congregation's support for the individual.

Activities and Discussion Questions

1. Attend a confirmation service of another faith. What differences do you perceive? Talk to the minister about the meaning of confirmation in his or her church. Discuss these different understandings in class.
2. What are the similarities between the meanings of confirmation and the meanings of baptism described in the previous chapter? In what sense are baptism and confirmation a single act and in what sense are they separate?
3. What is the importance of the act of laying on of hands in confirmation? What does this act symbolize?

4. What *really happens* to the candidate at the time of confirmation? How is the candidate different following confirmation?
5. What are the duties and privileges of membership other than the two mentioned on page 45?
6. What does it mean to receive the Holy Spirit in confirmation? How does this affect a person? How has the Holy Spirit helped you since your confirmation?
7. Write a one-sentence definition of confirmation and share it with others in a group.
8. If Jesus and others are reputed in the scriptures to have received the Holy Spirit without a specific confirmation ritual, why is it necessary today? Could people receive the Holy Spirit today without being confirmed? Explain.
9. Using concordances to the three books of scripture, look up all the references to confirmation that you can find (many are found in the endnotes in this chapter). What important concepts do you find?
10. Why is it important that confirmation be celebrated in a public worship setting? What is the role of the congregation in the confirmation service?
11. Suggest some ways that confirmation services can be made more meaningful to both candidate and congregation.
12. Is confirmation primarily a divine act or a human act? Explain.
13. Is initiation into the church complete after baptism? If so, what is the role of confirmation? If not, how does confirmation make the process complete?
14. What is the most appropriate time lapse between baptism and confirmation? What criteria are relevant when deciding this question in a specific case?

Notes

1. *Church Administrator's Handbook* (Independence, Missouri: Herald Publishing House, 1987), 39.
2. Doctrine and Covenants 52:3c.
3. Confirmation by one elder is permissible but it is customary to use two when they are available.
4. Doctrine and Covenants 17:8 establishes confirmation as the duty of the "elder," this term being interpreted to mean all members of the Melchisedec priesthood.
5. See for example in the Bible, Matthew 3:11 (3:38 IV), Acts 2:38 and 8:14-17, and Genesis 6:67-69 IV (accounts of Adam's baptism and confirmation are added to the biblical text at this point); Book of Mormon, II Nephi 13: 15-17, III Nephi 9:14-15; Doctrine and Covenants 17:8c (not included in pre-1835 published versions of this document), 17:8e, 34:2c, 39:6, 49:2g-h.
6. Doctrine and Covenants 17:8c, e; 17:18b; 32:3c; 34:2c; 39:6; 49:2h; 52:3c; 55:1b; 68:4a; 76:5c; in the Bible, Acts 8:18 and 19:6.
7. See chapter 4 for further discussion of the relationship between confirmation and partaking of the Lord's Supper.
8. Doctrine and Covenants 17:8c and e, 18:4d, 32:2g, 34:2c, 39:2b, 39:3c and 6, 49:2h, 68:4a, 83:10c; Book of Mormon, Mormon 3:33, III Nephi 5:46, 9:14, and 12:10 and 33; in the Bible, Acts 1:5 and 11:16, Genesis 6:68-69 (IV only), John 1:28 (IV only), Luke 3:16 (3:23 IV), Matthew 3:11 (3:38 IV), Mark 1:8 (1:6 IV).
9. Matthew 3:16 (3:45 IV), Mark 1:10 (1:8 IV), Luke 3:22 (3:29 IV).
10. John 1:9 NRSV.
11. Moroni 6:4.
12. Doctrine and Covenants 18:4d.
13. III Nephi 12:10.
14. Matthew 3:16-17 (3:45-46 IV), Mark 1:9-11 (1:7-9 IV), and Luke 3:21-22 (3:28-29 IV); see also John 1:32 (particularly verse 31 IV).
15. Acts 8:18 and 19:6.

CHAPTER 4

The Lord's Supper

The Lord's Supper is the most frequently and widely observed of the sacraments in the RLDS Church. Usually celebrated on the first Sunday of each month, it consistently draws a higher attendance than the weekly worship (usually preaching service). It is unique among the sacraments in that each member participates *directly* in the Lord's Supper on a repeated basis rather than only once in a lifetime as with baptism, confirmation, infant blessing, and the evangelist's blessing.

The following passage from the Doctrine and Covenants, originating in 1830, gives the basic procedure for the Lord's Supper.

> It is expedient that the church meet together often to partake of bread and wine in remembrance of the Lord Jesus; and the elder or priest shall administer it; and after this manner shall he administer it:
>
> He shall kneel with the church and call upon the Father in solemn prayer, saying, O God, the eternal Father, we ask thee in the name of thy Son Jesus Christ, to bless and sanctify this bread to the souls of all those

who partake of it, that they may eat in remembrance of the body of thy Son, and witness unto thee, O God, the eternal Father, that they are willing to take upon them the name of thy Son, and always remember him and keep his commandments which he has given them, that they may always have his Spirit to be with them. Amen.

The manner of administering the wine: He shall take the cup also, and say:

O God, the eternal Father, we ask thee in the name of thy Son Jesus Christ, to bless and sanctify this wine to the souls of all those who drink of it, that they may do it in remembrance of the blood of thy Son which was shed for them, that they may witness unto thee, O God, the eternal Father, that they do always remember him, that they may have his Spirit to be with them. Amen.[1]

This instruction is similar to that found in the Book of Mormon in which the prayers of blessing are word for word identical but preceded by the following:

The manner of their elders and priests administering the flesh and blood of Christ to the church: They administered it according to the commandments of Christ; wherefore we know the manner to be true, and the elder or priest administered it: And they knelt down with the church and prayed to the Father in the name of Christ, saying,...[2]

The Book of Mormon was published in March 1830, and so the procedures for the Lord's Supper were available in print to the membership from the time of the church's organization in April 1830. The text of what was later to become Section 17 of the Doctrine and Covenants was first published in the first issue of the first church periodical in June 1832.[3] Three key elements are identified in these procedures. First, the Lord's Supper is administered by priests or elders. Second, specific prayers of blessing are prescribed. Third, the minister and congregation kneel while the prayers are read. Each of these practices is normative for RLDS worship.

The customary procedure can be described as follows: The emblems are placed on the Communion table before the service of worship starts and are usually covered with a white cloth. Unfermented grape juice in individual glasses and bread are used. The bread may be broken into individual portions before being placed on the table or it can be broken as part of the ritual. When it comes to the point in the service for the Lord's Supper to be administered, the tablecloth is removed and the emblems are prepared (bread broken, vessels arranged). The congregation is then invited to kneel while a priest or elder reads the prayer on the bread (see preceding). After the people have returned to their seats, portions of bread are served to the ministers who are officiating in the service including the priests and elders who are to serve the congregation. Each person in the congregation is then served directly by one of the priests or elders.

Basically the same procedure is used for the wine: The prayer is read while everyone is kneeling; the ministers and then the congregation are served. Bread and wine remaining after all persons have been served are either returned to the Communion table or carried out of the sanctuary.

Questions have arisen from time to time about the degree of flexibility permitted in the basic practice. Whether the emblems should be blessed before or after they are broken and poured was apparently a matter of contention to which Joseph Smith III addressed these words found in Doctrine and Covenants 119:5d: "The officer may break the bread before it is blessed, and pour the wine before it is blessed; or he may, if he be so led, bless the bread before it be broken and the wine before it be poured." He obviously left the matter to the discretion of the presider. However, paragraph 5e of this same document does require that "both bread and wine should be uncovered when presented for the blessing to be asked upon it."

Another major question has related to the elements themselves. The first paragraph of Section 26 of the Doctrine and Covenants includes the following:

> For, behold, I say unto you, that it mattereth not what ye shall eat, or what ye shall drink, when ye partake of the sacrament, if it so be that ye do it with an eye single to my glory; remembering unto the Father my body which was laid down for you, and my blood which was shed for the remission of your sins; wherefore a commandment I give unto you, that you shall not purchase wine, neither strong drink of your enemies; wherefore ye shall partake of none, except it is made new among you; yea, in this my Father's kingdom which shall be built up on the earth.[4]

The first sentence is interesting in that it appears to grant considerable freedom in choice of emblems, rightly emphasizing the spirit of the occasion. However, the last part talks specifically about wine. This is the basis for the fairly widespread practice of using homemade, unfermented wine. In the context of admonition to avoid the use of "wine or strong drink" we read further "this [wine used for Lord's Supper] should be wine; yea, pure wine of the grape of the vine, of your own make."[5]

The 1913 General Conference took firm action against the use of fermented wine by adopting a resolution "that fermented wine should not be used in the Sacrament services of the church, but that either unfermented wine or water should be used, and so be in harmony with the spirit of the revelations."[6] This Conference action came in response to a question on the matter raised by the New South Wales, Australia, District.[7] The use of water is also referred to in the Doctrine and Covenants.[8]

Although the current practice of the church is to use either homemade or commercially produced grape juice, the door is open for the use of water or other liquids. These alternatives are rarely if ever used in the United States, Canada, Australia, New Zealand, and Great Britain. However, other liquids, such as the juices of berries and coconuts, are used in some countries where the church has representation. These are used because wine, grape juice, or water are either not readily available or are considered inappropriate to the specific cultural setting. Such practice is authorized by the following statement in the *Church Administrator's Handbook:* "Because grapes are not available in many parts of the world, substitutes appropriate to the symbol intended are permissible."[9]

There appears to have been no controversy over the use of bread. Home-baked or commercially produced bread of the kind one would normally eat at home is used. Individual portions are prepared by either cutting or breaking the sliced or unsliced bread into pieces usually about one-half inch square. On occasion larger pieces may be broken from a whole loaf and distributed in this form.

During the early days of the church the wine was served by using a common cup. The transition to the use of individual cups was, no doubt, gradual, and this form is now in general practice. The issue was dealt with at the 1915 General Conference which adopted a resolution submitted by the Massachusetts District.[10] This resolution says "that the individual Sacrament service be used throughout the church, as the authorized form of service, in conformity with the laws of health as prescribed by the health officials of the United States."[11] Although this seems to settle the matter rather decisively, a reading of the minutes of the Conference session at which the resolution was passed indicates otherwise. In the course of discussion on the motion the following question was addressed to the chair, at that time occupied by President Elbert A. Smith. "Would it be your interpretation that if this resolution passes...that any church or branch...not using the individual cup would not be using the authorized form?"[12] President Smith then replied, "The chair would understand that that would be the form having the approval and the authority of the church, but would not understand that any branch would be prohibited from using any other form."[13] This would appear to leave the door open for the use of the common cup, which is in fact used regularly in the church in some countries.

Other variations in practice occur from time to time. When circumstances permit and the congregation is small, participants may be invited to come forward to the Communion table to be served. The emblems may be brought to the table during the service as part of an offering. The bread and wine may be blessed before or after they are broken and poured; however, they should be uncovered before being blessed.[14]

The law of the church carefully prescribes who is eligible to administer the Lord's Supper. Responsibilities which are limited by law to the priest[15] or elder[16] are (1) reading the prayers of blessing[17] and (2) the serving of the emblems to the membership. The latter was clarified at the 1895 General Conference which approved a resolution stating "that the act of conveying the emblems to those partaking forms a part of the work of 'administering the sacrament,' and, under the law, neither teachers, deacons, nor laity have right to serve in that capacity."[18]

In the early years of the Latter Day Saint movement the Lord's Supper was served every Sunday.[19] Now, however, the general practice is to celebrate this sacrament on the first Sunday in each month, although nothing prohibits its more frequent occurrence as may be determined by local circumstances. Frequency was apparently a matter of contention in 1887 when Joseph Smith III gave the following instruction to the church:

> And the Spirit saith further: Contention is unseemly; therefore, cease to contend respecting the sacrament and the time of administering it; for whether it be upon the first Lord's day of every month, or upon the Lord's day of every week, if it be administered by the officers of the church with sincerity of heart and in purity of purpose, and be partaken of in remembrance of Jesus Christ and in willingness to take upon them his name by them who partake, it is acceptable to God.[20]

The practice of weekly celebration could be based on instruction given in 1831 which says, "Thou shalt go to the house of prayer and offer up thy sacraments upon my holy day."[21] This instruction goes on to say, "On this, the Lord's day, thou shalt offer thine oblations."[22] This is the basis for the practice of receiving a special oblation offering for the poor at each service in which the Lord's Supper is celebrated. This practice was reinforced at the 1917 General Conference which passed a resolution "that every branch should comply with the law by receiving oblations at Sacrament services, as found in Doctrine and Covenants 59:2."[23]

The custom of allowing time for members of the congregation to offer prayers and testimonies after partaking of the Lord's Supper was quite widespread at one time. President F. M. Smith discouraged this practice, however, and during the last generation it has been discontinued in most places. The reason is that Communion services tended to become quite tedious with persons bearing lengthy testimonies; the significance of the Lord's Supper itself became obscured.

It is traditional for the Lord's Supper emblems to be served to baptized members of the RLDS Church only. The 1868 General Conference passed a resolution spelling this out. It reads, "that unbaptized persons, whether children or adults, are not entitled to partake of the sacrament of bread and wine."[24] The minutes of that Conference[25] session give no detail about the circumstances which gave rise to the passage of this resolution or any discussion that occurred on the Conference floor. The assumption behind this resolution seems to be that a person baptized in another Christian denomination is regarded as "unbaptized" and therefore ineligible to receive the RLDS Communion.

It appears that this practice of "close" communion has been with the RLDS Church from its earliest years. In the Book of Mormon Jesus is recorded as saying, "Behold, there shall one be ordained among you, and to him will I give power that he shall break bread, and bless it, and give it to the people of my church, to all those who shall believe and be baptized in my name."[26] Also, "And this shall ye always do unto those who repent and are baptized in my name."[27] These verses clearly establish who is eligible to partake. The Inspired Version rendition of the Lord's Supper account in the twenty-sixth chapter of Matthew is also significant. The relevant verse reads (additions capitalized), "For this is IN REMEMBRANCE OF my blood of the new testament, which is shed for AS many AS SHALL BELIEVE ON MY NAME, for the remission of THEIR sins."[28]

It is quite likely that I Corinthians 11:23-29 served as an important image in the development of Latter Day Saint Communion practice in general and in the thought of Joseph Smith in particular.[29] The key concept here is that of worthiness (or unworthiness) to partake (see verses 27-29). Joseph Smith made no changes in the biblical text in these seven verses but we do find a parallel for them in the Book of Mormon as follows:

> And now, behold, this is the commandment which I give to you, that ye shall not suffer anyone knowingly to partake of my flesh and blood unworthily, when ye shall minister it, for whoever eateth and drinketh my flesh and blood unworthily, eateth and drinketh damnation to his soul.
>
> Therefore if ye know that a man is unworthy to eat and drink of my flesh and blood, ye shall forbid him; nevertheless ye shall not cast him out from among you, but ye shall minister to him and shall pray for him to the Father in my name.
>
> And if it so be that he repenteth and is baptized in my name, then shall ye receive him, and shall minister to him of my flesh and blood.[30]

An examination of these verses shows a direct link between one who is unworthy and one who is not baptized. It is assumed here that the unworthy person is not a baptized member. Note also the injunction not to cast unworthy people out. This is reinforced in a subsequent verse which says, "Ye shall not cast him [the unbaptized person] out of your synagogues, or your places of worship, for to such shall ye continue to minister."[31] This same basic concern is included in Doctrine and Covenants as follows. "Ye shall not cast anyone out of your sacrament meetings, who is earnestly seeking the kingdom; I speak this concerning those who are not of the church."[32] The concern here is that non-RLDS persons not be excluded from the service of worship in which the Lord's Supper was served as was the practice in the first-century church.

It should also be noted that III Nephi 8:61 says that "ye shall forbid him [the unworthy person]." The mechanics of how this is done have varied somewhat within the church. Although there have been times when the emblems have been withheld from some people who try to partake, this policy is discouraged. The last two decades have seen a significant degree of discussion on the church's policy of close Communion. The theological assumptions undergirding the official stance have been examined and attempts have been made by individuals and groups to strengthen or weaken the basic stance outlined in General Conference Resolution 91 (see preceding). As a result of debate at the 1974 World Conference, the First Presidency issued an interpretive statement that reaffirmed Resolution 91 and spelled out additional concerns which included, "In the administration of the service and of the rite itself, discretion is left to administrative officers and those presiding over the service." And, "We suggest care be taken that the administration of this sacred ordinance shall not become an occasion of violence against any unbaptized person present."[33] This statement provided for a somewhat flexible interpretation of Resolution 91 which, however, is still the official policy of the RLDS Church.

Another important question relates to eligibility of *members* to partake of the Lord's Supper. Doctrine and Covenants 46:1d says, "Ye are also commanded not to cast anyone, who belongeth to the church, out of your sacrament meetings; nevertheless, if any have trespassed, let him not partake until he makes reconciliation."[34] This acknowledges that the issue of worthiness does in fact apply to RLDS members as well as others. Paul said, "But let a man examine himself, and so let him eat of that bread, and drink of that cup."[35] This establishes a policy of self-imposed exclusion for people who feel that their unworthiness is a barrier to their participation in the Lord's Supper. The denial of the emblems by a minister to a member deemed unworthy has occurred on occasion but is contrary to official practice. The only exception is when a member has been excommunicated following trial in a church court. Such a member is not eligible to receive Communion until restored to full fellowship.

The reference to making reconciliation in Doctrine and Covenants 46:1d led in former years to the regular practice of public confession in the service of worship at which the Lord's Supper is served. This tended to become rather prolonged in some cases, causing a delay in the actual serving of the emblems. Thus, the injunction in Doctrine and Covenants 119:5f: "The bread and wine should be administered in the early part of the meeting, before weariness and confusion ensue." Public confession is now rarely found in RLDS Communion services. Neither is the passing of the peace or any other act of general reconciliation included as a regular part of RLDS worship.

Before concluding this section on eligibility, it is appropriate to deal with the question of whether the emblems are to be served to baptized members who have not yet been confirmed. The currently accepted practice within the church is that of confirming people before they partake of the Lord's Supper for the first time. The reason is that individuals are not considered full members of the church until they have been confirmed. This has not, however, always been the universally accepted practice. The following resolution was introduced to the 1893 General Conference:

> Whereas, There is no specific announcement in the law as to whether or not the sacrament may be administered to baptized but unconfirmed believers, and—
> Whereas, There appears to be a necessity that some general understanding be had in order to settle the question in many minds regarding the matter, therefore be it—
> *Resolved,* That priests of the Aaronic order, in all cases where necessity for decision exists, be authorized to act as the Spirit shall direct them.[36]

This resolution, although not adopted,[37] gives definite indication of the fact that policy on this matter was not well established. The resolution was introduced as a result of a question on the matter presented to the Conference the previous day.[38]

The basic law of the church found in the Doctrine and Covenants includes the statement:

> The elders or priests are to have a sufficient time to expound all things concerning the church of Christ to their understanding, previous to their partaking of the sacrament, and being confirmed by the laying on of the hands of the elders; so that all things may be done in order.[39]

This places the sacrament before confirmation but not in such a way that this order is established as a requirement. In Joseph Smith's history we read an account of where Joseph, his wife, John Whitmer, Newel Knight, and his wife held a meeting at Joseph's house. The account specifies that neither Joseph's nor Newel's wife had yet been confirmed. The report continues in part, "We partook together of the Sacrament, after which we confirmed these two sisters into the church."[40] If we think it inconceivable that the three confirmed members partook while denying the emblems to the others, we have a case where the Lord's Supper was served to unconfirmed persons. Nowhere in the scriptures, Conference resolutions, or in the official *Church Administrator's Handbook* is there to be found a specific rule on this matter. However, the general practice is that members are confirmed before receiving Communion. In fact, new members are often served first at the Communion service following their confirmation.

The Meaning of the Lord's Supper

In the RLDS Church, the Lord's Supper has several meanings. The most important are:
• remembrance of Jesus Christ
• celebration of Christ's contemporary presence
• renewal of the baptismal covenant
• confession and forgiveness
• expression of the unity of the fellowship

Remembrance

A major emphasis has traditionally been put on the remembrance aspect of the Lord's Supper. Numerous scriptural passages provide the basis for this.

In the Book of Mormon account of Jesus instituting the Lord's Supper we read: "And this shall ye do [administer bread] in remembrance of my body, which I have shown to you. And it shall be a testimony unto the Father that ye do always remember me. And if ye do always remember me, ye shall have my Spirit to be with you."[41] And with respect to the wine: "And this shall ye always do...in remembrance of my blood, which I have shed for you, that ye may witness to the Father that ye do always remember me. And if ye do always remember me, ye shall have my Spirit to be with you."[42] These particular passages appear to serve as the basis for the prayers of blessing[43] quoted in full on pages 53-54 of this book. These prayers emphasize the remembrance function of the Lord's Supper.

The Inspired Version of the Bible exhibits noteworthy additions to the Gospel texts at this point. In Luke 22 the major manuscripts disagree[44] as to whether or not the second half of verse 19 and all of verse 20 should be in the text. The Revised Standard Version includes these as a footnote but the King James Version includes them in the body of the text. A comparison of the text with I Corinthians 11:24-25 shows the possibility of these lines being a later addition based on the already existing Pauline text. Joseph Smith, in working with the King James text, retains these lines without change. He also adds the concept of remembrance found in I Corinthians 11:25 and Luke 22:19 to the texts of Matthew and Mark which he makes to read (added words capitalized):

> And as they were eating, Jesus took bread and brake it, and blessed it, and gave to HIS disciples, and said, Take, eat; this is IN REMEMBRANCE OF my body WHICH I GIVE A RANSOM FOR YOU. And he took the cup, and gave thanks, and gave it to them, saying, Drink ye all of it. For this is IN REMEMBRANCE OF my blood of the new testament, which is shed for AS many AS SHALL BELIEVE ON MY NAME, for the remission of THEIR sins. AND I GIVE UNTO YOU A COMMAND-MENT, THAT YE SHALL OBSERVE TO DO THE THINGS

WHICH YE HAVE SEEN ME DO, AND BEAR RECORD OF ME EVEN UNTO THE END.[45]

And as they did eat, Jesus took bread and blessed it, and brake, and gave to them, and said, Take IT, AND eat. BEHOLD, this is FOR YOU TO DO IN REMEMBRANCE OF my body; FOR AS OFT AS YE DO THIS YE WILL REMEMBER THIS HOUR THAT I WAS WITH YOU. And he took the cup, and when he had given thanks, he gave it to them; and they all drank of it. And he said unto them, This is IN REMEMBRANCE OF my blood which is shed for many, AND the new testament which I GIVE UNTO YOU; FOR OF ME YE SHALL BEAR RECORD UNTO ALL THE WORLD. AND AS OFT AS YE DO THIS ORDINANCE, YE WILL REMEMBER ME IN THIS HOUR THAT I WAS WITH YOU AND DRANK WITH YOU OF THIS CUP, EVEN THE LAST TIME IN MY MINISTRY.[46]

These scriptural passages provide the basis for the major emphasis on the remembrance aspect of the Lord's Supper that has characterized the Latter Day Saint tradition. Remembrance in this context emphasizes the atoning or sacrificial work of Christ as illustrated by such phrases as "in remembrance of my body which I give a ransom for you" and "in remembrance of my blood...which is shed" found in the Matthew accounts. Remembrance also refers to Christ's presence as in the phrase "ye will remember this hour that I was with you" found in the Mark account and the phrase "this do in remembrance of me" found in the Luke and I Corinthians accounts.

Christ's Contemporary Presence

Emphasis on Christ's presence in the Lord's Supper has tended to take a backseat to the dominant theme of remembrance just discussed. Although the presence of Christ in the Lord's Supper would not be denied by most RLDS members, it is not emphasized either. This is probably due to the fact that any interpretation coming close to the doctrine of physical presence (transubstantiation) as traditionally advocated by Roman Catholics and others would be vigorously rejected by most Latter Day Saints.

A study of the appropriate scriptural texts is informative at this point. Joseph Smith's changes in the Matthew and Mark passages quoted in the previous section do more than simply inject the concept of remembrance into the text. The change in Matthew 26:22 from "this is my body" to "this is IN REMEMBRANCE OF my body" and in verse 24 from "this is my blood" to "this is IN REMEMBRANCE OF my blood" serve to eliminate the direct reference to the bread and wine as the body and blood, a literal view of the physical presence of Christ in the elements. The same result is brought about by equivalent changes in Mark 14:21 and 23. It is interesting to note that Joseph Smith did not make corresponding changes in the Luke account[47] or in the I Corinthians account.[48] Both of these accounts contain the words "this is my body." The reference to the wine, however, is less direct, using the words, "this cup is the new testament in my blood."[49]

This inconsistency shows up in other places on this same subject. In the Book of Mormon (published earlier than the Inspired Version) we read, "Ye shall not suffer anyone knowingly to partake of my flesh and blood unworthily, when ye shall minister it, for whoever eateth and drinketh my flesh and blood unworthily, eateth and drinketh damnation to his soul."[50] This verse, which has clear parallels to I Corinthians 11:27-29, shows an interesting structure. Whereas the I Corinthians rendition includes no direct references to the bread and wine as being the body and blood, the

Book of Mormon account includes two such direct references followed by two more in the next two verses.

One Doctrine and Covenants reference is pertinent to this discussion. The earliest published version of Section 17 includes the following verse: "An apostle is an elder, and it is his calling to baptize, and to ordain other elders, priests, teachers, and deacons, and to administer the flesh and blood of Christ."[51] In two subsequent publishings of this section, it is changed to read, "...and to administer the BREAD AND WINE—THE EMBLEMS OF THE flesh and blood of Christ."[52]

The quotations cited here do not seem to provide sufficient evidence to show a change in the thought of Joseph Smith or of the church regarding the nature of the bread and wine. It seems likely instead that the variations and changes reflect a rising consciousness on the part of Joseph Smith as to the implications of certain phrases. In other words, although he may have referred to the bread and wine as the body and blood in some cases[53] it is likely that he used these words symbolically. Later, however, he may have realized that these words implied something that he did not mean and so therefore made changes.[54]

There is, however, indication that in the Reorganization (post-1852 church) the view of the bread and wine has undergone some modification. The 1875 General Conference passed the following resolution:

> WHEREAS, Believing that the bread and wine used at the sacrament are simply blessed for the use of those who at the time and with an understanding of its purpose partake of it, in no way relating to its subsequent use, therefore be it
> *Resolved*, That we rescind a former resolution of General Conference making necessary the passing of the bread until all be taken.[55]

Although a survey of the preceding resolutions does not find the resolution rescinded by this action, the April 15, 1868, issue of the *Saints' Herald* includes the following item in a column written by President Joseph Smith III.

> In administering the sacrament, the elders are hereby instructed to prevent the desecration of the ordinance by a waste of the bread blessed upon the occasion. —A very proper way of preventing this, is, if more is prepared than is used at one passing, pass until all is used. It is urged by some, that not unfrequently the bread which is left is thrown aside, when after becoming dry it is thrown out and wasted. This ought not to be. For thereby a disregard to the ordinance may be engendered in the minds of some, who otherwise would revere it.[56]

This reference together with the resolution referred to is sufficient to establish that it was indeed the practice to pass the bread until all was consumed. No mention, incidentally, is made of the wine. It should be noted that in Joseph Smith III's statement, the concern is as much for avoiding waste as it is for the desecration of the sanctified element.

The adoption of the 1875 resolution would seem to indicate a change in the way the bread and wine are viewed. The earlier practice would seem to imply that once the emblems are blessed they remain "sanctified"[57] and designated for a purpose and therefore should be totally consumed. This practice may also be based on the biblical injunction, "Drink ye all of it."[58] The current view suggests that the emblems are blessed only for the occasion and that the method of disposition of the unused portions is of little consequence. The 1948 injunction of President Israel A. Smith is, however, usually followed: "The use to which left-over bread and wine may be put after the service should not reflect an undignified attitude toward them."[59]

It is also relevant to note the practice regarding the serving of the emblems to shut-ins. In the statement by Israel Smith it is suggested that although permissible it is certainly not necessary to repeat the prayers of blessing in the presence of people not in attendance at the service at which the emblems were blessed. The decision is left to the presiding officer.[60] It seems reasonable to conclude that the prayers of blessing relate more to the occasion and worship setting in which the emblems are administered than they do to the nature of the emblems themselves.

The emblems have, it seems, always been considered symbols. They play a vital role, however, in the Lord's Supper. In Latter Day Saint thought, the emblems serve not *as* the presence of Christ in a literal or physical sense but rather as vehicles that help make possible Christ's presence within the worshiping community. This presence is made possible in a unique way through the symbolic power of the elements.

Covenant "Renewal"

An important meaning attached to the Lord's Supper in the RLDS Church is the "renewal" of the baptismal covenant. Some people who object to the idea of covenant *renewal* because they see the baptismal covenant as a one-time act prefer to think in terms of the reaffirmation or even remembering of the baptismal covenant. Although there appears to be no specific scriptural basis for viewing the Lord's Supper in relationship to the baptismal covenant, the understanding of baptism as commitment to follow Christ and the idea of the Lord's Supper as remembering Christ make this link understandable. The prayers of blessing on the emblems point to important elements of the covenant. In particular, the phrases "witness unto thee, O God, the eternal Father, that they are willing to take upon them the name of thy Son, and always remember him and keep his commandments which he has given them" indicate the nature of the covenant element of the Lord's Supper. The covenant is one of allegiance, memory, and obedience to Christ.

This understanding of covenant and its renewal is a major explanation for the practice of close Communion. In other words, it is an act in which members share in the renewal (or reaffirmation) of a unique covenant. Although members of other Christian churches have been baptized according to the beliefs and procedures of those churches, members of the RLDS Church share a covenant with God that is in a particular institutional setting and allegiance. This line of reasoning has at times caused some members to adopt an arrogant stance in which they see the RLDS Church as having exclusive claim to the sacraments rightly administered. Nevertheless, it is usually claimed that the Lord's Supper as practiced in the RLDS Church has a significance for Reorganized Latter Day Saints that it is unlikely to have for anyone else. This is based on interpretation of the Lord's Supper as renewal or reaffirmation of the baptismal covenant.

In recent years there have been discussions in the church over the pros and cons of discontinuing the practice of close Communion. The issue hinges centrally on whether the Lord's Supper is seen primarily as a distinctive mark of RLDS identity, being tied closely to an understanding of baptism as membership in a particular church, or as a mark of commonality shared by all Christians, being tied closely to an understanding of baptism as membership in the wider "body of Christ."

Confession and Forgiveness

The Lord's Supper provides an opportunity for members of the church to reflect back over their past in an attitude of repentance and confession. They assess the extent to which they have lived up to the demands of their baptismal covenant. Paul admonished his hearers: "Examine yourselves, and only then eat of the bread and drink of the cup. For all who eat and drink without discerning the body, eat and drink judgment against themselves."[61]

Time for public or private confession is sometimes provided within the service of worship at which the Lord's Supper is administered. This gives individuals opportunity to acknowledge their sinful condition and lay themselves at the mercy of God. In this setting, many testify of experiencing God's forgiveness and reconciliation. The partaking of the emblems then grants the person anew the presence of Christ, freeing them for new opportunity to faithfully execute the responsibilities of their covenant discipleship.

Unity of the Fellowship

The symbolism of the bread as the body of Christ has added meaning when seen in light of Paul's description of the church as Christ's body.[62] The Lord's Supper is the occasion where *together, as a corporate body*, the church involves itself in an act of special significance. Members partake in the presence of each other and are witnesses to each other's action. The Lord's Supper is an important occasion in which the unity of the church is celebrated.

The Lord's Supper also serves to sustain the church. By partaking symbolically of Christ's body and blood, the church is nourished and sent forth again to be witnesses of God's redeeming action in the world. Participation with others in this sacred rite acknowledges the joint responsibility of all who claim the name of Christ.

Planning the Service of the Lord's Supper

The following suggestions are offered for consideration by those whose responsibility it is to plan Communion services.

1. *The Communion message* centers on the essentials of the Lord's Supper itself and its meaning in the life of the church in general and the specific congregation in particular. This is no place for discourses or admonitions on topics unrelated to the sacrament. The Lord's Supper is important enough that the entire service should be focused on it. The Communion message is best kept to ten or at most fifteen minutes. In other words, it should not be confused with the traditional thirty-minute RLDS sermon. The message draws directly on the scriptural base for the Lord's Supper, especially that found in the following references: Doctrine and Covenants 17:22 and 17:23; Book of Mormon, III Nephi 8:32-42, Moroni 4 and 5; Bible, Matthew 26:26-29 (26:22-26 IV), Mark 14:22-25 (14:20-25 IV), Luke 22:14-20, and I Corinthians 11:23-29. One or more of these scriptures will often be read in connection with the Communion message. The message may focus also on the theme selected for the day, but not at the expense of ignoring the Lord's Supper.

2. *The Communion service* is especially meaningful if planned according to the structure of the elements of

worship described in the introduction to this book. Following the expressions of praise and thanksgiving that begin a service of worship, the mood of repentance and confession is particularly appropriate in preparation for the Lord's Supper itself. We should be reconciled to our brothers and sisters before partaking of the emblems. This mood might be expressed through the use of congregational hymns such as numbers 103-119 in *Hymns of the Saints* or through prayer offered by one individual on behalf of the congregation or in unison by the congregation.

In addition, allowing thirty to forty-five seconds of silence for private prayer and meditation is an excellent way of providing opportunity for expressions of confession and repentance. It is important that some expression of God's forgiveness be included either along with the chosen expression of confession or immediately following. Hymns expressing forgiveness are listed in the topical index to *Hymns of the Saints*. An appropriate scripture also could express forgiveness. The concept of self-examination is found in Paul's writings in I Corinthians 11:27-29 already referred to.

3. *Preparation* for receiving the emblems is an important element of the worship experience. In addition to the mood of confession and the response of forgiveness mentioned, preparation can also take the form of expressions of solidarity and unity among the fellowship. The Lord's Supper is an act of the corporate body, so the congregation needs to feel and express its unity. One method of expressing unity is what is traditionally termed "passing the peace." This has early Christian origins but has generally not become a part of RLDS worship. At an appropriate time in the service, before the blessing and serving of the emblems and following

a signal from the presiding minister, individuals turn and shake the hand of, or embrace, people whom they can reach without moving from their place. The physical gesture may optionally be accompanied by a verbal greeting such as, "May the peace of God be with you." Such expressions seem quite unusual and possibly inappropriate to those who are unaccustomed to them. However, they have the potential of significantly enriching the worship experience and of beautifully expressing the corporate and dependent nature of our lives. Other expressions of corporate unity can be found in hymns such as numbers 325-345 emphasizing the Lord's Supper and numbers 290-295 emphasizing the church. Appropriate scripture passages and prayers can also serve this purpose.

4. *The actual Lord's Supper itself* can appropriately be seen as a fourfold act as expressed in Matthew 26:26 (verse 22 IV). *First,* Jesus TOOK the bread. The custom among early Christians was to *bring* the bread and wine as part of the offertory at an appropriate point in the service. The symbolism of the people bringing the gifts, of everyday foodstuffs, is significant. Such a practice might, on occasion, be used today. When the emblems are arranged on the table before the service begins, attention can be drawn to the act of taking by the uncovering of the emblems before the Communion message. This allows the person delivering the message to bring the elements more directly to the consciousness of the congregation.

Second, Jesus BLESSED, or GAVE THANKS for, the elements. The term "Eucharist" means giving thanks. The prayers, found in Doctrine and Covenants 17:22 and 17:23 and also in Moroni 4 and 5, are appropriately offered in a spirit of thanksgiving. This mood of thanksgiving might be further expressed by the use of a hymn, prayer, or statement of thanksgiving just before the reading of the prayers. To remind the congregation of the words of the prayers and their meaning as they are being read, the prayers might be printed in the bulletin or called to the attention of members in the front of *Hymns of the Saints* so they might follow the words as they are being read. Reference to the words of the prayers during the Communion message is also helpful.

Third, Jesus BROKE the bread. It is customary to leave part of the bread unbroken when the tables are prepared so it can be broken as part of the preparation of the elements before serving. This symbolism is important in calling attention to the brokenness of Christ's physical body as he was persecuted and finally crucified. A whole loaf, broken in two or more pieces at the appropriate time, can also serve as a dramatic symbol of this aspect of Communion. When the Lord's Supper is being served in small congregations, it may be particularly appropriate to start with just a whole loaf and break off enough pieces to serve the congregation. Corresponding symbolism with the wine can be demonstrated by having on hand a pitcher of grape juice that is subsequently poured into individual glasses. The pouring of wine symbolizes the spilling of the blood of Christ.

Fourth, Jesus GAVE the bread and wine to his disciples. In the RLDS tradition it is customary to serve members of the congregation in their seats. An alternative is to invite the congregation to come forward to the Lord's table to receive the emblems. If the details are carefully thought through, this can be done even in large congregations. The symbolism of coming to the table can be meaningful as a response to Christ's invitation to eat and drink with him. With small congregations it might be possible to have the congregation sit around one or more tables for the entire Communion service. Where disposable paper cups are used or where some arrangement is made for gathering reusable cups after the service, it can be a meaningful symbol of congregational unity if members of the congregation partake of the elements at the same time rather than the usual custom of partaking when each person is served.

5. *A number of actions* are appropriate after the Lord's Supper itself has been served. These include moments of silent prayer and meditation; prayers, hymns, or scriptures of dedication, response, and commitment; statements of challenge and commission to the congregation; the offertory, including oblation; pastoral prayer; prayer of benediction or sending forth statement.

6. *Special care* must be taken when other sacraments such as infant blessings and confirmations are included in the service of the Lord's Supper. This may dilute the meaning and experience of both sacraments and make the service too long. Where circumstances dictate the wisdom of including additional sacraments in the service, this should be done only after careful planning and not as a last-minute expediency.

7. *One meaningful custom* in some places in the church is to serve newly baptized members before other members of the congregation are served. This is usually handled by the presiding minister who moves from the rostrum and serves the new member(s) in their seats after making verbal announcement of what is being done, calling the new member(s) by name.

Activities and Discussion Questions

1. Carefully read the prayers used for blessing of the emblems. What do they say and mean? Which phrases seem to be most significant to you?

2. Think carefully through the procedure used in the administration of the Lord's Supper in the RLDS Church. What is the significance of each act?

3. Which of the following departures from traditional practice would you be comfortable with at least on occasion? Why or why not? Which might be permissible in cultures other than that with which you are familiar?

   a. Prayers of blessing read in unison by congregation.

   b. One combined prayer of blessing offered over both bread and wine.

   c. Members of the congregation moving from their seats to the Communion table to receive the emblems.

   d. Drinking from a "common" cup passed around the congregation.

   e. Use of water in place of "wine."

   f. Use of "other juices" in place of "wine."

4. Do you think that baptized but unconfirmed people should be eligible to partake of the Lord's Supper emblems? Why or why not? What does your answer imply about an understanding of baptism, confirmation, church membership, and the Lord's Supper itself?

5. How do you interpret the statement, "It mattereth not what ye shall eat, or what ye shall drink, when ye partake of the sacrament" (Doctrine and Covenants 26:1b)? What limits would you place on the kind of elements that can be used?

6. How often would you like to see the Lord's Supper served in your congregation? What might be the advantages and disadvantages of celebrating the Lord's Supper more frequently than once each month?

7. What role does the oblation have in the Communion service? How could it be made more meaningful?

8. Would you favor the serving of the Communion emblems to the unbaptized children of members? What would be the advantages and disadvantages of such a procedure? How about non-RLDS spouses?

9. Would you favor openly serving the Communion emblems to people who are not members of the RLDS Church? Why or why not? What would be the advantages and disadvantages of such a procedure? What does your answer say about your understanding of the meaning of the Lord's Supper and of the church?

10. Review the discussion of unworthiness on pages 60-63. Do you see the scriptures on this subject as applying mainly to yourself, to other members, or to non-RLDS people? How and by whom is worthiness decided? On what grounds does a presiding officer or member of the priesthood have the right to withhold the emblems from a person?

11. What role do you see repentance (or confession) and forgiveness having in the Lord's Supper service? How is the former expressed and the latter received?

12. Which of the five meanings discussed on pages 65-74 are most important to you? Why?

13. How is the presence of Christ experienced in the Lord's Supper? What specific acts make this presence real to you?

14. What aspects of Christ's ministry do you "remember" most in the Lord's Supper?

15. What do you see as the difference between renewing, reaffirming, and remembering one's baptismal covenant in the Lord's Supper? Which word most closely describes your understanding?

16. What do you feel is the most appropriate way to dispose of the leftover elements after the service? Why?

17. Attend Lord's Supper services in other churches (Roman Catholic, Lutheran, Methodist, Mormon). Note the differences in procedures. If possible invite the ministers of the churches you visit to explain how they view the Lord's Supper.

18. After you have participated in a Lord's Supper service, what do you feel has happened to you? How are you different? What benefits have you received?

19. What is the meaning of the breaking of the bread and of the pouring of the wine? Are they important to the ritual of the Lord's Supper?

Notes

1. Doctrine and Covenants 17:22-23; see also 17:8b, 10a, and 11e.
2. Moroni 4:1-3; see also III Nephi 8:32-42 for the Book of Mormon account of Jesus' institution of the Lord's Supper.
3. *The Evening and the Morning Star* 1, no. 1 (June 1832): 1.
4. Doctrine and Covenants 26:1b-d (August 1830).
5. Doctrine and Covenants 86:1c (February 27, 1833).
6. *Rules and Resolutions*, 1990 Edition (Independence, Missouri: Herald Publishing House, 1990), GCR 702 (adopted April 9, 1913).
7. *General Conference Minutes* (April 8 and 9, 1913): 1701 and 1717.
8. Doctrine and Covenants 119:5c.
9. *Church Administrator's Handbook* (Independence, Missouri: Herald Publishing House, 1987), 61.
10. *General Conference Minutes* (April 8, 1915): 2028-2029.
11. *Rules and Resolutions*, GCR 747 (adopted April 8, 1915).
12. *General Conference Minutes* (April 8, 1913): 2029.
13. Ibid.
14. Doctrine and Covenants 119:5d-e.
15. Ibid., 17:10a.
16. Ibid., 17:8b.
17. The matter of whether the congregation may audibly join the minister in the recitation of the prayers is open to question.
18. *Rules and Resolutions*, GCR 401 (April 12, 1895).
19. See *A Brief History of the Church of Christ of Latter Day Saints* by John Corrill (St. Louis, 1839), 47; and *History of the Church of Jesus Christ of Latter Day Saints; Period 1: History of Joseph Smith, the Prophet by Himself*, edited by B. H. Roberts (Salt Lake City, Utah: Deseret News, 1904), vol. II, 408.
20. Doctrine and Covenants 119:5a-b.
21. Ibid., 59:2f (August 7, 1831).
22. Ibid., 59:2h.
23. *Rules and Resolutions*, GCR 773 (adopted April 10, 1917).
24. Ibid., GCR 91 (adopted April 9, 1868).
25. *General Conference Minutes* (April 9, 1868): 140.
26. III Nephi 8:32.
27. Ibid., 8:40.
28. Matthew 26:24 IV; see Matthew 26:28 KJV.
29. For additional significance of this and other scriptural passages quoted in this section, see the section of this chapter that deals with meaning (pages 65-74).
30. III Nephi 8:60-62.
31. Ibid., 8:64.

32. Doctrine and Covenants 46:2 (March 8, 1831).

33. "The Lord's Supper" by the First Presidency, *Saints Herald* 121, no. 12 (December 1974): 5.

34. Doctrine and Covenants 46:1d (March 1831).

35. I Corinthians 11:28.

36. *General Conference Minutes* (April 11, 1893): 66.

37. Consideration of the motion was "indefinitely postponed" (Ibid.).

38. Ibid., 65.

39. Doctrine and Covenants 17:18b.

40. *History of the Church of Jesus Christ of Latter Day Saints* Vol. I (Deseret News: 1902), 106 and 108.

41. III Nephi 8:34-36.

42. Ibid., 8:40-41.

43. Book of Mormon, Moroni 4:4 and 5:3; and Doctrine and Covenants 17:22 and 17:23.

44. See *Gospel Parallels* edited by Burton H. Throckmorton, Jr. (Nelson, 1957), 166.

45. Matthew 26:22-25 IV (corresponds to Matthew 26:26-28 KJV). Note that the IV puts the breaking of the bread before the blessing, and the KJV has the order reversed.

46. Mark 14:20-24 IV (corresponds to Mark 14:22-24 KJV).

47. Luke 22:19.

48. I Corinthians 11:24.

49. Luke 22:20 and I Corinthians 11:25.

50. III Nephi 8:60.

51. *Book of Commandments* (1833), chapter 24, verse 32, and *The Evening and the Morning Star* 1, no. 2 (June 1832): 1.

52. *The Evening and the Morning Star* (reprint) (January 1835): 1; and Doctrine and Covenants 17:8b (1835).

53. For example in III Nephi 8:60 and Moroni 4:1.

54. For example in Doctrine and Covenants 17:8b.

55. *General Conference Minutes* (April 9, 1875): 299, since known as GCR 172.

56. *Saints' Herald* 13, no. 8 (April 15, 1868): 122.

57. See prayers of blessing, Doctrine and Covenants 17:22 and 17:23.

58. Matthew 26:27 KJV (verse 23 IV).

59. *Saints' Herald* 95, no. 3 (January 17, 1948): 4.

60. *Church Administrator's Handbook* (Independence, Missouri: Herald Publishing House, 1987), 62.

61. I Corinthians 11:28-29 NRSV.

62. I Corinthians 12.

CHAPTER 5

Blessing of Children

The sacrament of blessing recognizes the entrance of a new life into the church community. In situations where a child is blessed soon after being born, it may be appropriate to view the blessing as the first step in that individual's initiation into the church. In other words, for such children to be seen as "joining" the church at baptism does not give appropriate recognition to their having been affiliated with the church since birth. For this child, baptism is a second step in the initiatory process. For people whose first affiliation with the church occurs after they are eight years of age, baptism is the first initiatory step. Blessing, then, is seen as an "interim" rite for the benefit of those who are not yet old enough to be baptized.

Children from birth to the eighth birthday are eligible for blessing. Normally children of church members are brought for blessing some time during the first six months after birth. It is not unusual, however, for older children to be blessed. This happens if the parents join the church when the child is older or if circumstances are such that a child of members was not blessed earlier (if the family lived far away from a congregation of the church). Blessing is available to children regardless of whether or not the parents are members of the RLDS Church. It is usual, however, for the parents to be instructed in the meaning of the sacrament before the blessing is performed.

The 1913 General Conference of the church passed a resolution saying "that the ordinance of blessing should not be administered to children who are old enough to be baptized."[1] Before this time there was no recognized age limit above which a child should not be entitled to the ordinance of blessing.[2] Apparently there were on record cases of twelve-year-olds, even fourteen-year-olds, being blessed before this date.[3]

A blessing is administered by the laying on of hands by elders. The only reference in the entire Doctrine and Covenants to this rite says, "Every member of the church of Christ having children, is to bring them unto the elders before the church, who are to lay their hands upon them in the name of Jesus Christ, and bless them in his name."[4] The customary procedure is for two elders[5] to officiate. One elder usually holds the child in his arms and the other offers a prayer of blessing with his hands laid on the child. Occasionally a blessing will be performed with the child being held by a parent, or by the child sitting on a chair or on the lap of a parent. No specific words are prescribed for inclusion in the prayer. Customarily the blessing of children is administered within the context of a regular Sunday worship service. This appears to have been the procedure from the beginning of the RLDS Church.

The blessing of children is based primarily on the Gospel accounts of Jesus receiving and blessing children,[6] particularly the Mark account which says, "And he took them [children] up in his arms, put his hands upon them, and blessed them."[7] The blessing of children is also part of the ministry of Jesus found in the Book of Mormon: "[Jesus] took their little children, one by one, and blessed them, and prayed to the Father for them."[8] It is important to note that in the Book of Mormon account the practice of laying on of hands is not mentioned at all in connection with the blessing of children. Together with the Doctrine and Covenants passage mentioned in the preceding section, we see that the rite of blessing is mentioned in all three books of RLDS scripture. It is also noteworthy that neither the Bible nor the Book of Mormon records the practice of blessing by individuals other than Jesus.

Blessing symbolizes and demonstrates God's love and concern for the child. It recognizes the birth of a new individual who is unique and has worth in God's sight. In blessing, the parents, ministers, and congregation recognize human dependency on God as the source and strength of life. God is requested to care for the child and to provide the Holy Spirit to guide and strengthen the child as he or she grows.

Bringing a child for blessing is the decision of the parents. As such it is their recognition of responsibility for the care and nurture of the child. The parents' visual presence, standing near while the blessing is performed, symbolizes their commitment to providing the kind of environment in which the child can grow to maturity with faith and responsibility. This commitment is made to God and to the church community assembled in worship.

The prayer of blessing requests guidance not only for the child on whom hands are laid but also for the parents in their specific responsibility. Recognition of the congregation's responsibility for the child is frequently also explicit in the prayer. In the blessing the church community welcomes the child into fellowship and acknowledges its role in the child's nurture. The congregation offers its support to the parents in their role and also assumes responsibility of its own as an extended family.

The inclusiveness of this sacrament is phrased appropriately by Brockway and Yale: "The purpose is...that the special help of God is invoked for the nurture of the whole personality, including emotional, spiritual, moral, and physical development."[9]

The practice of blessing children soon after birth and of baptizing them at the age of eight years raises an important question regarding the status of the unbaptized child. The Book of Mormon, Doctrine and Covenants, and Inspired Version of the Bible all speak to this question. The basic position is that little children are "whole," incapable of sin, without need for repentance, and are saved without baptism. The Doctrine and Covenants puts it this way:

> Little children are redeemed from the foundation of the world, through mine Only Begotten; wherefore they cannot sin, for power is not given unto Satan to tempt little children, until they begin to become accountable before me.[10]

Several biblical passages peculiar to the Inspired Version have an important bearing on this question also. In Matthew 18, in the context of Jesus' discussion of people becoming as little children,[11] the following words are found which are not in other versions: "These little ones have no need of repentance, and I will save them."[12] Then in chapter 19 of Matthew, we read (IV additions capitalized): "Then were there brought unto him little children, that he should put his hands on them and pray. And the disciples rebuked them, SAYING, THERE IS NO NEED, FOR JESUS HATH SAID, SUCH SHALL BE SAVED."[13] The last part of this verse has obvious reference to chapter 18, verse 11 referred to above.

These verses from the Inspired Version rendition of Matthew form an important basis for Latter Day Saint belief and practice regarding children.

To these verses can be added another reference peculiar to the Inspired Version, this time from the Old Testament. As part of the long section on the life and teachings of Enoch inserted between Genesis 5:21 and 22 of the King James Version we read:

> And the Lord said unto Adam, Behold, I have forgiven thee thy transgression in the garden of Eden. Hence came the saying abroad among the people, that the Son of God hath atoned for original guilt, wherein the sins of the parents cannot be answered upon the heads of the children, for they are whole from the foundation of the world.[14]

A Book of Mormon instruction reads, "Ye must repent, and be baptized in my name, and become as a little child, or ye can in nowise inherit the kingdom of God."[15] This verse is similar in substance to the reference from Matthew cited earlier. The implication is that baptism makes one "as a little child" and that such little children are qualified to "inherit the kingdom of God." The most extensive Book of Mormon statement on the subject under discussion is, however, found in the book of Moroni.[16] The key verses read as follows:

Little children are whole, for they are not capable of commiting sin; wherefore the curse of Adam is taken from them in me that it hath no power over them; and the law of circumcision is done away in me.[17]

Teach parents that they must repent and be baptized, and humble themselves as their little children, and they shall be saved with their little children; and their little children need no repentance, neither baptism.[18]

Little children are alive in Christ, even from the foundation of the world.[19]

All children are alike to me; wherefore I love little children with a perfect love; and they are all alike, and partakers of salvation.[20]

Little children cannot repent;...they are all alive in [God] because of his mercy.[21]

All little children are alive in Christ.[22]

Planning the Service of Blessing

The following suggestions are offered regarding the service of blessing:

1. The blessing of a child is, like other sacraments, an important event in the life of the child, the family, and the church. For this reason the service of worship should be planned with the blessing as the focal point. Services of blessing are ideally scheduled for a time and place that permits and encourages the members of the congregation to be present.

Adding a blessing to an already scheduled preaching or other type of service suggests hasty, last-minute planning, which is likely to demean the sacrament and the occasion on which it is celebrated. The number of blessings performed at any one service should be kept to a minimum.

2. Involve the child's entire family in the service of worship. This may include brothers and sisters, grandparents, and others as well as the child's parents.

Members of the family could be asked to read scripture, offer prayer, share in testimony, or participate in some other way. These people may also be involved in the planning of the service.

3. A short statement regarding the meaning of the sacrament of blessing is an important part of the service. This statement needs to bear the spirit of thanksgiving to God whose creative nature is expressed in the birth of a child. Attention will also be given to the role of the child in the context of both family and church. The parents and the congregation are charged with the nurture and care of the child. This statement is accompanied or preceded by an appropriate scripture reading.

4. Following this statement, a response from the child's family and the congregation is appropriate. One or both of the parents might make such a response. In addition, if the responses are short, a sister, brother, or grandparent might also respond. The congregation's response could be made by an individual representative or by using a unison reading or carefully chosen hymn. Responses of this kind might occur before the blessing itself or after it.

5. It is customary for the parents to bring the child forward to the rostrum and to stand close by while the blessing is taking place. Other family members (grandparents, sisters, brothers) could also be invited to come forward with the parents.

6. Following the blessing, acts of dedication and commitment are appropriate. One or more of the following could be used: offertory, response (as in item 4), hymn, prayer, scripture reading, pastoral statement.

7. The congregation may wish to present a gift to the child and family as a symbol of remembrance of the occasion. A well-chosen book, certificate, or other ap-

propriate object could serve this purpose. The presentation could be made before the conclusion of the service.

8. At the close of the formal part of the service, members of the congregation may wish to greet the child and family. A "receiving line" might serve this function as might an informal reception held in an adjacent room.

Activities and Discussion Questions

1. Attend a service of blessing in an RLDS congregation. What did you observe? What was the role of (a) the child, (b) the ministers, (c) the parents, and (d) the congregation? What was said in the prayer? What role did the blessing play in the whole service of worship?

2. What is the significance of the practice of blessing children regardless of whether or not their parents are members of the RLDS Church? What might be reasons for blessing only the children of members?

3. What kind of instruction should be given to the parents of children who are blessed? Why is this instruction needed?

4. What is it about the sacrament of blessing that makes it unnecessary for people over eight years of age? Is it appropriate to regard blessing as an "interim" rite? What value might there be in blessing children over eight?

5. What is the parents' role in the blessing of their child? What promises or commitments do they make? What blessings do they receive?

6. To what extent is it appropriate to view the parents as the recipients of the blessing rather than or in addition to the child?

7. How is the rite of blessing part of a person's initiation into the church?
8. What do you think are the most important functions or benefits of the blessing?
9. What actually happens in the lives of children when they are blessed? How are they different from children who are not blessed or different from how they were before they were blessed? What is the nature of the blessing received?
10. Prepare orders of worship for a service of blessing. Discuss the orders in a group. Are all parts of the service related to the sacrament of blessing itself? How is the congregation involved?
11. What different things do you think should be contained in the prayer of blessing?
12. What should be the role of the congregation in the sacrament of blessing?
13. What about a blessing makes it unnecessary for the rite to be repeated several times as a child grows?
14. How do you react to the view of children as "whole," incapable of sin, without need for repentance, and saved without baptism? Reread the scriptures referred to on pages 88–89 if you wish. Does this understanding of children square with your experience and with your beliefs about God?
15. Read Moroni 8:5-29 in its entirety. How do you react to those verses that speak out against those people who deny the understanding of the status of children being expressed in this passage?
16. Attend a service of infant baptism at a Roman Catholic church or other church where it is practiced. In what ways is this rite similar to and different from blessings in the RLDS Church in both procedure and meaning?

Notes

1. *Rules and Resolutions, 1990 Edition* (Herald Publishing House, 1990), GCR 701.
2. *General Conference Minutes* (April 9, 1913): 1707.
3. Ibid.
4. Doctrine and Covenants 17:19.
5. Construed to mean any member of the Melchisedec priesthood.
6. Matthew 19:13-15, Mark 10:13-16 (11-14 IV), and Luke 18:15-17.
7. Mark 10:16 (verse 14 IV).
8. III Nephi 8:23.
9. Charles E. Brockway and Alfred H. Yale, *Ordinances and Sacraments of the Church* (Herald Publishing House, 1962), 136.
10. Doctrine and Covenants 28:13a.
11. Matthew 18:2 IV.
12. Ibid., 18:11 IV.
13. Ibid., 19:13 IV. Compare the same verse in other versions.
14. Genesis 6:55-56 IV.
15. III Nephi 5:40.
16. Moroni 8:5-29.
17. Moroni 8:9. Compare Doctrine and Covenants 28:13a quoted above.
18. Moroni 8:11.
19. Ibid., verse 13.
20. Ibid., verse 18.
21. Ibid., verse 20.
22. Ibid., verse 25.

CHAPTER 6

Ordination

The sacrament of ordination is the procedure by which calls to specific ministry in the church are both recognized and accepted in the lives of individuals. It is the rite by which certain ecclesiastical privileges and responsibilities are conferred.

Ordination is an act of the corporate body. The church proclaims that God has called specific individuals to fulfill certain functions and that the membership of the church is willing to accept the ministry of these people. Ordination grants the authority to perform certain duties. This authority is given to the individual by God and also by the church.

In ordination individuals accept the responsibilities of the office to which they have been called and dedicate their lives to ministering on God's behalf. Ordination gives the individual the authority to act for God and the church in certain specified responsibilities.

The concept of *authority* can be distinguished from that of *power*. With regard to priesthood, authority means that when members are ordained the church is granting them the right to perform certain acts (administration of sacraments). By granting authority the church agrees to accept the validity of these acts. Power, on the other hand, means that God gives the ordained the capability to perform these same acts, which they otherwise could not do. Although Latter Day Saints have emphasized authority in priesthood, an understanding of power, in this regard, has by no means been absent. Ordained people traditionally have been seen to have the God-given power to perform the acts that ordination grants them the authority to do.

Another way of illustrating the distinction between authority and power is to talk in terms of *external* authority and *internal* authority. Ordained members, by virtue of being ordained to certain offices, have the external authority to perform certain functions. Internal authority, on the other hand, is evidenced by the manner in which persons perform these functions. Matthew 7:29 KJV reads, "For he [Jesus] taught them as *one* having authority, and not as the scribes." Clearly the scribes had external authority, but Jesus had internal authority. Jesus' authority was recognized by those who witnessed his ministry. However, Jesus did not have what was accepted by many as external authority in his day. This suggests the possibility that internal authority may be resident within individuals who do not have external authority.

Ordained individuals make their most significant contributions to the church when their ministry combines both the external and internal dimensions of authority.

The prominence of responsibility over privilege is important to an adequate understanding of ministry.

People are ordained so they can serve God and the church. The spirit of "I can do this and you can't" (or "You can do this and I can't") is contrary to the intent of ordination and may render the efforts of the minister ineffective. The affirmation, "All are called according to the gifts of God unto them,"[1] provides the general context of ministry in which the role of each ordained person is seen. The call to discipleship, which comes to *all* people, is the most important calling a person can receive. Acceptance of this call is evidenced by baptism and membership in Christ's body. The ordained person acts to enable the ministry of the entire body rather than acting as *the* minister.

In harmony with the RLDS understanding that God is self-revealing in every day and time, the church has always emphasized the initiative of God in the calling and ordination of people to occupy ministerial roles within the church. The process leading to ordination begins with the appropriate church administrative officers identifying what they understand to be the call of God to individuals.[2] Joseph Smith and other early Latter Day Saint leaders believed strongly that God had called them to assist in "a great and marvelous work."[3] Further scriptural basis for this view is found in Hebrews 5: "One does not presume to take this honor, but takes it only when called by God."[4]

The importance of God's call in the ordination procedure must be seen in light of the church's understanding of itself as called and directed to perform God's redeeming ministry in the world. The call of people to accept the rights and responsibilities of ordination is one of the tangible evidences that God leads and directs the church today. It is the specific expression of a wider principle.

God's call is also important in terms of the church's understanding of how an ordained minister functions. Ordination grants an individual the right and responsibility to perform certain ministerial functions which, if performed by an unordained person, would not be acceptable to the church. These include administration of church sacraments and serving as the pastor of a local congregation. Only one who is called and ordained according to accepted procedures can legitimately act in these capacities.

It should be said at this point that many other Christian denominations also understand ordination in terms of a call from God. The distinction is in who *initiates* (or in other words, identifies and acts on) the call. In the RLDS Church the call is initiated by someone who has already been called and ordained to act on God's behalf. In many other denominations individuals recognize God's call to themselves and then proceed to qualify for ordination by processes of formal education and other denominationally established procedures.

Although God's call is primary in the ordination process in the RLDS Church, the individual's own sense of call is also important. Some people accept the call to be ordained only after they feel personal assurance that God has indeed called them. Others accept as a result of faith in the process by which calls originate or out of a sincere desire to serve.

Formal education has never been a prerequisite to ordination. The call of God has been seen by some as superior to formal education, even to the extent of claiming that God's call is all that a person needs to minister effectively. However, in recent years church leadership has placed increasing emphasis on formal education as an important tool for the ordained. This was made explicit in 1984 with the following words from President Wallace B. Smith: "Let specific guidelines and instructions be provided by the spiritual authorities, that all may be done in order."[5] This led to the publication of *Guidelines for Priesthood* by Herald House in January 1985.[6] Included is a section on "Priesthood and Education" which outlines preordination expectations and continuing education expectations. While not rigidly enforced, such expectations are one of the topics included in the triennial review process for each priesthood member—a process inaugurated in 1985.

The Structure and Functioning of Priesthood

There are two orders of priesthood in the RLDS Church and several offices within each order. These are the Melchisedec and Aaronic priesthoods. They are described in detail in a document presented by Joseph Smith, Jr., to a council of church leaders held in Kirtland, Ohio, on March 28, 1835.[7]

As explained in this document, the Melchisedec priesthood is named after Melchisedec who is referred to as "priest of the most high God" in Genesis.[8] In Hebrews 5 Christ is referred to as "a priest forever after the order of Melchizedek."[9] In the Inspired Version Melchisedec is described as having been "ordained a priest after the order of the Son of God."[10] Additional references to the Melchisedec priesthood are found in the Doctrine and Covenants.[11]

The Aaronic priesthood is named after Aaron, companion of Moses. Aaron and his sons were designated to "minister unto me in the priest's office."[12] The fifth chapter of Hebrews already referred to also describes Aaron as being called of God.[13] This priesthood is also referred to as the Levitical priesthood,[14] and even the "lesser" priesthood as contrasted to the "greater" (Melchisedec) priesthood.[15]

The Melchisedec priesthood exercises administrative responsibility and ministers in "spiritual things"[16] including the administration of the sacraments of the church.[17] The Aaronic priesthood ministers in temporal affairs and in some cases administers "outward ordinances"[18] including baptism and the Lord's Supper.[19] Discussion of the duties of each priesthood office is found in chapter 5 of *The Priesthood Manual* (Herald House, 1990).

Most priesthood offices are mentioned in the Bible.[20] However, it is by no means clear that these designations actually refer to offices or what their duties were. Restoration as applied to priesthood refers to the *concept* of priesthood in general rather than to particular offices, duties, or organizational pattern.

Procedures for Calling and Ordination

Calls to offices within the priesthood are initiated by pastors and district, stake, regional, and World Church administrators. Calls are submitted to higher administrative officers for clearance before the person to be ordained is told of the call. If the person accepts the call, it is then submitted to a conference of members for their approval. Upon acceptance by the appropriate jurisdictional conference, the ordination is authorized. This practice is based on the statement that, "No person is to be ordained to any office in this church, where there is a regularly organized branch of the same, without the vote of that church."[21]

In the early days of the church ordination was permitted without conference authorization in places where branches of the church did not exist.[22] This applied, however, only to the ordination of members to the Aaronic priesthood and to the office of elder. Ordination to the high priesthood required authorization by a high council or General Conference.[23] More complete details regarding these procedures are found in *Church Administrator's Handbook.*[24]

Ordination is by the laying on of hands and spoken prayer. Ordination to the Aaronic priesthood is usually by elders or high priests but may be by Aaronic priests. Ordination to the office of elder is by other elders or by high priests. Ordination to the high priesthood is by high priests. Two or more officiants usually take part in the rite, but it is permissible for only one to ordain if another qualified person is not available. Chapter 3 of the Book of Moroni in the Book of Mormon describes the ordination procedure:

> The manner which the disciples, who were called the elders of the church, ordained priests and teachers: After they had prayed to the Father in the name of Christ, they laid their hands upon them, and said, "In the name of Jesus Christ I ordain you to be a priest (or if he be a teacher, I ordain you to be a teacher) to preach repentance and remission of sins through Jesus Christ by the endurance of faith on his name to the end. Amen."
>
> And after this manner they ordained priests and teachers, according to the gifts and callings of God to men; and they ordained them by the power of the Holy Ghost, which was in them.

Although the words to be spoken are specified here, the church today does not require that these or any other specific words be used. That the church continues to use the specified words prescribed for the Lord's Supper but not these for ordination can probably be accounted for in part by the fact that the former were reiterated in the Doctrine and Covenants but the latter were not.

A license certifying the office to which a person is ordained is issued following the actual ordination. This is a small card that can be carried in one's billfold.

Ordination in the RLDS Church is to a specific calling and office. Individuals may occupy one office from the time of ordination until death or may be ordained to one or more additional offices during their lifetimes.

There is, in practice, a fair degree of mobility between offices within the two orders. Most people ordained to the Melchisedec order occupy one or more offices within the Aaronic priesthood first. Some might be ordained a deacon, then a teacher, and then a priest. Others may be ordained directly from deacon to priest or perhaps be ordained a teacher or priest without ever occupying the office of deacon.

A large percentage of people ordained to the Aaronic priesthood are, after a period of time, ordained to the office of elder in the Melchisedec priesthood. Many occupy this office for the rest of their lives although some are subsequently ordained to the office of seventy or one of the offices within the high priesthood (all those occupying the office of high priest, bishop, evangelist, apostle, or president).

The church does not like to think of hierarchy in priesthood or that a person is promoted from one office to another. This is counterproductive to the intent of ordination and leads to false expectations. However, there has been a temptation to view the offices as deacon, teacher, priest, elder, and high priest in ascending order. A person occupying any office is authorized to perform all duties in "lower" offices. Also, one of the duties of each office is to assist people occupying "higher" offices when occasion requires. Thus, the teacher "is to take the lead of meetings in the absence of the elder or priest"[25] and the priest is to "assist the elder if occasion requires."[26] However, this does *not* mean that teachers or deacons can administer sacraments.[27] Neither can priests administer those sacraments that use the laying on of hands (except to ordain other members of the Aaronic order).

Ordination to any office is valid until death or ordination to another office. The following categories exist to which each priesthood member is assigned, regardless of office held:

1. *Active*: The person is active in appropriate areas of ministry.
2. *Inactive*: The person still holds the office but is inactive.
3. *Superannuation*: The person is retired from active ministry.
4. *Release*: The person relinquishes the privileges of the office.
5. *Suspension*: The person's activity in the office is temporarily suspended.
6. *Silence*: The person's priesthood privileges are revoked.

More complete descriptions of these categories and the grounds and procedures for individuals being assigned to them are found elsewhere.[28]

Requirements for Ordination

In addition to the call from God described earlier, several other considerations are important to the calling and ordination of priesthood in the RLDS Church.

Before 1985 only men were ordained to the priesthood. Some members within the church viewed this as an expression of God's will that remains valid across time and culture. Others viewed it as a culturally determined policy originating in times when women held no leadership roles in church or society. During the 1970s and early 1980s in particular, challenges to the established policy arose. The 1976 World Conference culminated its spirited debate on the issue by rescinding a 1905 resolution which said, "Resolved, that we...do not now see our way clear to report favorably upon ordination of women."[29] The 1976 resolution is as follows:

> Whereas, Resolution 564, adopted April 18, 1905, is no longer responsive to the needs of the church; and
>
> Whereas, A limited number of recommendations for women to be ordained to the priesthood have been submitted through administrative channels, and
>
> Whereas, We are restricted from processing these under the provisions of Resolution 564 arrived at by common consent; and
>
> Whereas, After research, consultation, and prayerful consideration of many factors, we find no ultimate theological reason why women, if it were thought wise to do so, could not hold priesthood; and
>
> Whereas, Acceptability by those to whom ministry is offered is a significant factor and to some extent would be determined by existing cultural and sociological conditions; therefore be it
>
> *Resolved,* That Resolution 564 be rescinded; and be it further
>
> *Resolved,* That consideration of the ordination of women be deferred until it appears in the judgment of the First Presidency that the church, by common consent, is ready to accept such ministry.[30]

Part of the action approving this resolution also provided for the inclusion of an additional letter of explanation in the official *Conference Bulletin*. This letter, written by the First Presidency, ended with these words:

"The First Presidency have no intention to approve the ordination of women until the World Conference takes some action to provide for it."[31]

Some delegates to the 1980 World Conference wanted to be sure that such a change would not be forthcoming. They introduced a resolution, "That women shall not be ordained to the priesthood in the Reorganized Church of Jesus Christ of Latter Day Saints."[32] When this resolution was brought up for consideration, an objection to consideration was sustained[33] and the matter was not discussed.

The debate intensified at the 1982 World Conference. The Jefferson City District submitted a resolution, "That the World Conference declare itself an inappropriate body for initiation of consideration of ordination of women, and...That the Conference wait upon prophetic guidance before consideration of this matter."[34] Halfway through Conference week—before the above resolution was acted on—a group of delegates prepared a resolution, "That this church affirms it will have no legislative or administrative barrier to ordination based on race, ethnic or national origin, or gender, for whomever God chooses to call through proper authority and procedure."[35] On the same day the First Presidency published a "Statement on the Role of Women" that concluded with the words, "We recommend that the resolutions before us on Ordination of Women...be laid on the table."[36] When the matter was called up for discussion toward the end of the week, the motion to lay on the table was lost and the Conference passed a resolution to refer the matter to the First Presidency to supervise the work of a task force to study the matter and report back to the 1984 World Conference.[37]

In this context of considerable interest and strong feelings on both sides, President Wallace B. Smith presented a document to the 1984 World Conference that authorized the ordination of women.[38] After considerable debate in quorum sessions and on the Conference floor, the document was approved and ordered to be included in the Doctrine and Covenants.

Since 1985 several thousand women have been ordained to various offices in the RLDS priesthood. An overwhelming majority of congregations in most countries where the church is located have both men and women ordained ministers. Although the impact of this change in policy is still being felt, it is safe to say that the action of ordaining women in the RLDS Church has prompted major controversy and contention on the one hand but has also enriched and expanded the ministries of ordained individuals in significant ways.

There is no minimum age requirement for ordination to the priesthood. Teenagers are frequently ordained to offices within the Aaronic priesthood and occasionally to the office of elder. Occasionally high priests will be ordained under the age of thirty, but this is somewhat unusual.

Ordination in the RLDS Church is based on qualifications and need. "Every elder, priest, teacher, or deacon, is to be ordained according to the gifts and callings of God unto him."[39] The expression or potential for ministry, as perceived by the administrative officer initiating the call, is an important element as is the need for personnel to perform specific ministries in a given local setting. At the end of 1991 there were more than 19,000 priesthood members out of the total listed membership of about 245,000.

Courses of study for preordination training are available through Temple School but few RLDS ministers receive training at accredited theological schools before they are ordained. In recent years ordained members who work full time for the church have received some theological education as part of their in-service training. The volunteer priesthood member is still, however, for the most part quite limited in ministerial training. Local jurisdictions offer classes, and some correspondence courses are available from Headquarters. These courses are twofold. First, they provide general orientation in denominational history, theology, and policy. Second, they instruct candidates in the duties of the office to which they are being ordained.

It is expected that the ordained follow a strict ethical code. All RLDS members are counseled to avoid habitual use of tobacco and alcohol.[40] In the case of priesthood members, such use results in the authority to function being removed by silencing. In all respects ordained people are expected to conduct themselves in a manner befitting ministers of Jesus Christ.

Planning the Ordination Service

The following suggestions are offered for planning ordination services.

1. It is particularly important that ordinations occur in a public worship setting. The congregation consists of those to whom the ordinand will provide ministry and those whom the ordinand will serve. The calling of one person to priesthood is symbolic of the call of all people to ministry. The service of worship should be focused on the meaning of calling and ordination. It is inadvisable to add ordinations to services that have been

planned with another focus in mind. As a general rule not more than four people should be ordained at any one service of worship.

2. A statement to the candidate will be presented by one of the ministers. This statement properly emphasizes the servant nature of priesthood and may refer to the ordained person's role as enabler of the ministry of others. Ordination to priesthood is not a call to position and privilege and should not be so depicted in this "charge." The statement is normally accompanied or preceded by an appropriate scripture reading.

3. A statement addressed to the congregation is also appropriate to the ordination service. This may be contained in the statement addressed to the candidate or in a separate one. Here the congregation is challenged to support the ordinands in their responsibilities and to receive the ministry that they will offer.

4. Ordinands usually have opportunity to share briefly their acceptance of the call and their desire to serve at the business meeting at which the call is approved. However, a short statement acknowledging human weakness and dependency on God and expressing a desire to serve is appropriate in the context of the ordination service itself. This statement properly belongs after the charge and will probably be placed before the ordination itself. Under certain circumstances, however, it may follow the ordination.

5. The statement addressed to the congregation invites response. This response may be offered in unison by the congregation or by a selected representative. The intent is that some verbal commitment is given by the congregation and received by the ordinand. This response may precede or follow the ordination itself.

6. A brief statement of welcome to the priesthood could be presented by an ordained member of the congregation.

7. The presentation of an appropriate book or other useful or symbolic item might be made to the newly ordained person following the ordination itself.

8. The ordinands can also read scripture, offer prayer, or participate in the service in some other way.

Activities and Discussion Questions

1. Write out a single-sentence definition of "ordination" and share it with others in a group.
2. Invite one or more ministers of other denominations to explain how ordination is carried out in their churches. Ask them questions about the *meaning* of ordination.
3. What does ordination *mean* to you? How are people different after they have been ordained?
4. What are the important prerequisites to effective ministry? How important are (a) God's call, (b) sincerity and dedication, (c) skill, (d) study and other preparation, (e) ordination?
5. Ask your pastor or someone else with experience to tell how calls to the priesthood are processed. What would you consider to be sufficient evidence that God had called someone to the priesthood?
6. How important is it to you whether or not all the priesthood offices in the church can be shown to be identical in function to those in biblical or Book of Mormon times?
7. What ecclesiastical acts are restricted by church law to certain priesthood offices (indicate your reference)? Which are performed by priesthood out of

tradition rather than church law? Which do you think should be reserved for priesthood? Why?

8. What are some specific ways that unordained people can offer ministry? What are some specific ways that ordained people can enable the ministry of the unordained?

9. Discuss the pros and cons of requiring certain training before a person can be ordained. What kind of training would you favor?

10. Research the procedure for calling members to the priesthood found in the *Church Administrator's Handbook* (1987), page 42, and *The Priesthood Manual* (1990), pages 143-166.

11. What would be your advice to individuals who feel strongly that they have been called by God to certain offices in the priesthood, have waited patiently several years for the calls to come, but nothing has yet resulted?

12. What would be the advantages and disadvantages of the use of prescribed words in prayers of ordination such as those described in the third chapter of Moroni?

13. Do you feel it inappropriate to view the priesthood structure as an order of progression as described on page 102? Why or why not? If not, how could this view be played down?

14. What do you regard as adequate reasons to place an ordained person under silence? Review the silencing procedures described on pages 49-51 of the *Church Administrator's Handbook* (1987). Do you believe this is fair to the ordained person and the church?

15. Review the procedure for priesthood reviews found on page 46 of the *Church Administrator's Handbook*

(1987) and discuss the pros and cons of this process. What changes would you recommend?

16. Would there be merit in ordination being valid only for a specified period of time or for ministry only in the church jurisdiction that has voted to approve the person's ordination? What would be the advantages and disadvantages of such a procedure?

17. Review the concepts of *power* and *authority* discussed at the beginning of the chapter. See also the description that follows that discussion regarding external and internal authority. Is this distinction important? Give examples of each concept.

Notes

1. Doctrine and Covenants 119:8b.
2. See pages 100-103 for more information on this procedure.
3. Doctrine and Covenants 6:1a.
4. Hebrews 5:4 NRSV.
5. Doctrine and Covenants 156:9d.
6. The principal sections of these guidelines are now included in *The Priesthood Manual* (Independence, Missouri: Herald Publishing House, 1990).
7. Doctrine and Covenants 104; see also 68:2.
8. Genesis 14:18 KJV (14:17 IV). The name of the priesthood in the RLDS Church usually follows the Doctrine and Covenants spelling, "Melchisedec," rather than the Old Testament spelling, "Melchizedek."
9. Hebrews 5:6. IV spelling here is "Melchizedek"; see also Hebrews 5:10 and 6:20.
10. Ibid., 7:3.
11. See Doctrine and Covenants 104.
12. Exodus 28:1, 3, 4, 41.
13. Hebrews 5:4.
14. Hebrews 7:11; and Doctrine and Covenants 104:1a and 2.
15. Doctrine and Covenants 104:8a-b.
16. Ibid., 104:3b.
17. Ibid., 17:8-9.
18. Ibid., 104:8b.

19. Ibid., 17:10.
20. In most cases there are far too many biblical references to list even in endnotes. The interested student can consult a complete Bible concordance.
21. See Doctrine and Covenants 17:16a.
22. See Ibid., 17:16b.
23. See Ibid., 17:17.
24. *Church Administrator's Handbook* (Independence, Missouri: Herald Publishing House, 1987), 42-46.
25. Doctrine and Covenants 17:11c.
26. Ibid., 17:10e.
27. Ibid., 1711e.
28. See *The Priesthood Manual* (1990), 168-172; and *Church Administrator's Handbook* (1987), 46-51.
29. Conference Resolution 564 (adopted April 18, 1905).
30. Conference Resolution 1141 (adopted April 1, 1976).
31. *World Conference Bulletin* (Friday, April 2, 1976): 265-266.
32. Ibid., (Tuesday, April 8, 1980): 274.
33. Ibid., 307.
34. Ibid., (Sunday, March 28, 1982): 268.
35. Ibid., (Wednesday, March 31, 1982): 331.
36. Ibid., (Wednesday, March 31, 1982): 337.
37. Ibid., (Saturday, April 3, 1982): 355.
38. Doctrine and Covenants 156:9c-d.
39. Ibid., 17:12a.
40. Ibid., 86:1b and 1d.

CHAPTER 7

Marriage

Less than a year after the official organization of the Latter Day Saint movement, Joseph Smith, Jr., presented an inspired document that said in part, "Marriage is ordained of God."[1] From the very beginning the state of marriage has been regarded with high esteem and the wedding ceremony featured as one of the important rites of the RLDS Church.

The basic procedures governing performance of the marriage ceremony were laid down in a document approved unanimously by a General Assembly meeting on August 17, 1835, in Kirtland, Ohio.[2] This document, now known as Section 111 of the Doctrine and Covenants, has appeared in every printing of this book by the Reorganized Church since the first edition of 1835.[3] The procedures outlined in this document have never been rescinded or replaced. They continue to serve as the basis for marriage in the church. The basic understandings and provisions of this document are as follows:

1. The church recognizes that marriage is subject to legal provisions established by various nations and states.[4] This aspect of marriage makes it unique among the sacraments of the church.

2. Marriages within the church should be solemnized in a public meeting of some kind.[5] This usually occurs in the context of a service of worship.

3. Marriages within the church are to be performed by members of the Melchisedec priesthood or by Aaronic priests.[6] It should be noted that marriage is *not* included as a duty of the priesthood in Section 17 of the Doctrine and Covenants where other duties are listed. This might mean that procedures for marriage were not well defined in the earliest years of the church. Neither teachers, deacons, nor laity are authorized to officiate at a marriage ceremony in the church.

4. The church recognizes the marriages of people who choose to be married by authorities outside the church.[7] This may be by civil authorities or ministers of other faiths. Recognition of this kind is based on the understanding that marriage is regulated by provisions of the state as described in item 1.

5. Paragraph 1d of Doctrine and Covenants Section 111 states:

> We believe that it is not right to prohibit members of this church from marrying out of the church, if it be their determination so to do, but such persons will be considered weak in the faith of our Lord and Savior Jesus Christ.

The phrase "marrying out of the church" has been interpreted to refer to marriage by other authorities as indicated above. This is the logical interpretation when seen in the context of the preceding part of paragraph 1. Another interpretation, however, is that it refers to marriage between a member of the RLDS Church and a person who is not a member.[8]

RLDS members are frequently discouraged from marrying a non-RLDS person because of the high probability that they will cease active participation in the church. On the other hand, many members are successful in bringing their spouses into active participation in the church and even into membership.

6. Certain procedures within the marriage ceremony itself are prescribed. Specifically the minister shall say, calling the man and woman by name, "You both mutually agree to be each other's companion, husband and wife, observing the legal rights belonging to this condition; that is, keeping yourselves wholly for each other, and from all others, during your lives?"[9] When they have answered affirmatively, the minister pronounces them "husband and wife" in the name of Christ and by authority of the state.[10] An additional benedictory statement is often added as follows: "May God add his blessings and keep you to fulfill your covenants from henceforth and forever. Amen."[11]

7. A record of each marriage is kept at Church Headquarters and also by the local recorder.[12]

8. "All legal contracts of marriage made before a person is baptized into this church, should be held sacred and fulfilled."[13] This again relates to the legal dimensions of marriage referred to in items 1 and 4.

9. Monogamy is the only form of marriage endorsed by the church, and polygamy is denounced.[14]

10. Individuals whose spouses have died are free to remarry.[15] Remarriage in cases of divorce is not dealt with in Doctrine and Covenants 111 and so will be discussed later in this chapter.

115

The Meaning of Marriage

Marriage within the church is considered to be a sacrament. The following understandings establish its sacramental character.

1. The act and state of marriage have their origins in the scriptures as being instituted by God. In Genesis we read, "And the Lord God said, It is not good that the man should be alone; I will make an help meet for him,"[16] and "Therefore shall a man leave his father and his mother, and shall cleave unto his wife; and they shall be one flesh."[17] The basic statement in the Doctrine and Covenants is as follows:

> Whoso forbiddeth to marry, is not ordained of God, for marriage is ordained of God unto man; wherefore it is lawful that he should have one wife, and they twain shall be one flesh, and all this that the earth might answer the end of its creation; and that it might be filled with the measure of man, according to his creation before the world was made.[18]

2. Not only is God seen as endorsing marriage in principle; divine action is also evident in each specific union of two people in the marriage ceremony. Doctrine and Covenants 111 indicates that after vows have been exchanged, the minister "shall pronounce them 'husband and wife' in the name of the Lord Jesus Christ."[19] In the Bible Jesus is recorded as saying in connection with marriage and divorce, "What, therefore, God hath joined together, let no man put asunder."[20] In the marriage ceremony the minister acts on behalf of God in joining together a man and a woman.

3. Marriage is a covenant. The covenant is made between the two individuals in the presence of God and of the church as witnesses. The words, "You both mutually agree to be each other's companion"[21] indicate

the nature of the marriage covenant. It is a commitment to companionship, mutual support, shared responsibility, and love toward each other. The marriage covenant has as its ideal the depth and integrity that characterize God's covenant relationship with humanity. The sacramental nature of the marriage covenant derives from its relationship to God's covenant with humanity. Furthermore, in marriage two individuals embark on a covenant relationship in which they commit themselves to express their best understanding of the demands of Christian discipleship.

Marriage in the RLDS Church is considered a lifelong commitment as indicated by the phrase, "during your lives,"[22] which is required as a part of each wedding ceremony in the church. This understanding of marriage as a lifelong commitment is the reason why divorce is to be avoided.[23] Before Joseph Smith's death in 1844 speculation regarding the eternal nature of marriage was present within the church. The origins, nature, and identification of the proponents of this view are beyond the scope of this study and remain the subject of historical inquiry. Suffice it to say that the Reorganized Church has always rejected the view that marriage covenants are valid after death. One might suppose that speculation about eternal marriage is based in part at least on Jesus' statements that "whatsoever thou shalt bind on earth shall be bound in heaven"[24] and "in the resurrection they neither marry, nor are given in marriage."[25]

Additional emphases in the church's understanding of marriage can be identified as follows:

4. The marriage relationship is unique. Part of the marriage vow reads as follows: "Keeping yourselves wholly for each other, and from all others, during your

lives."[26] This statement suggests that spouses enjoy a depth of relationship with and commitment to each other that surpasses that which characterizes their relationships with other people. Even though this phrase has usually been interpreted as prohibiting extramarital sexual relationships, it is broader than this. It suggests that spouses hold each other's interests and welfare uppermost when they make decisions regarding the use of their time, money, and other resources. Extremely flexible interpretations of the statement run the risk of violating the spirit of the marriage relationship. However, extremely literal interpretations run the same risk. A view of marriage that denies spouses the opportunity for interaction with other people stunts their growth as individuals seeking fulfillment in all aspects of their lives.

5. The church has always stood adamantly opposed to adultery. In the same spirit as the Ten Commandments,[27] modern-day scripture admonishes the church, "Thou shalt not steal; neither commit adultery, nor kill, nor do anything like unto it."[28] Adultery is seen as a flagrant violation of the marriage covenant. It represents one of the few grounds for expulsion from the church. Individuals who are guilty of adultery are counseled to repent, in which case they are forgiven. But if they commit adultery again they can be expelled from the church.[29]

The statement in the Doctrine and Covenants that "All legal contracts of marriage made before a person is baptized into this church, should be held sacred and fulfilled"[30] has interesting implications for situations where polygamists request baptism into the church. Such situations have arisen in the church and were the basis for some spirited discussion at the 1972 World

Conference. Inspired instruction to the church at that time included the affirmation, "Monogamy is the basic principle on which Christian married life is built."[31] Then, with obvious reference to polygamists who had recently been baptized in India, the document continued:

> Yet, as I have said before, there are also those who are not of this fold to whom the saving grace of the gospel must go. When this is done the church must be willing to bear the burden of their sin, nurturing them in the faith, accepting that degree of repentance which it is possible for them to achieve, looking forward to the day when through patience and love they can be free as a people from the sins of the years of their ignorance.[32]

The practice since that time is to continue to baptize polygamous individuals. However, if they marry additional wives after having been baptized this is regarded as adultery and grounds for expulsion from the church.

6. The church authorizes remarriage by church authorities following divorce in certain circumstances. The 1884 General Conference recognized the need for the establishment of criteria by which a divorced member might remarry within the church (by RLDS ministers). This began a process whereby, following each divorce, a report was filed and a decision made as to the eligibility of the respective parties to be remarried within the church. This process has been discontinued in recent years. The 1884 statement said, "Resolved...in case of separation of husband and wife, one of which is guilty of the crime of fornication, or adultery, the other becomes released from the marriage bond, and if they so desire may obtain a divorce and marry again."[33]

Over the years, as the incidence of divorce in society has become more frequent and the grounds for it broader, the church has responded by extending remarriage privileges to a wider range of people. The 1884 stance was modified in 1896 by addition of a provision relating to "abandonment without cause."[34]

A more flexible position on remarriage of divorced people was adopted by the 1962 World Conference and includes the following:

> The church recognizes that the remarriage of an innocent party in a divorce action is permissible when a divorce has been secured for any of the following reasons: adultery, repeated sexual perversion, desertion, such aggravated conditions within the home as render married life unbearable for the party petitioning or for the children of the marriage.[35]

This resolution goes on to say:

> Though the civil court may have accepted proof of lesser indignities as sufficient grounds for divorce, permission for remarriage should be granted only when the conditions complained of were of such an extreme nature as to place the other members of the family in serious and continuing jeopardy.[36]

Judgment of one of the parties in a divorce as guilty and the other as innocent implies a simplistic distinction that can rarely, in practice, be made. Recognizing this problem, the 1984 World Conference replaced the 1962 resolution with one that includes the following:

> Remarriage of a person whose previous marriage has been terminated should be approached with the same careful consideration and preparation as that appropriate for every marriage. In cases where the previous marriage was terminated by legal action the officiating minister should insure that marital preparation will include an exploration of the factors that characterized the marital history.[37]

The requirement of the formal report including details of the divorce has been dropped in favor of a simple report of the divorce date which is entered on the records at Church Headquarters.

Planning the Wedding Service

When planning wedding services the following suggestions might be found useful.

1. The bride, groom, and officiating minister play important roles in the wedding service. But the congregation is also important and should be active in the service. Congregational hymns, readings, and prayers make this possible. In addition to participation by the whole congregation, representatives of the congregation could be asked to offer prayer, read scripture, or make brief statements.

2. The bride, groom, and minister can benefit from working together on the planning of the wedding service. This provides the engaged couple the opportunity to include certain favorite scriptures and music in the service and also to compose their own vows if they wish. The minister can provide guidance as to what elements would combine to make the occasion dignified and worshipful.

3. The husband and wife may play different roles in a marriage but they are equal rather than one being subordinate to the other. Language and actions suggestive of inequality between the marriage partners should be avoided. For example, the inclusion of the injunction to "obey" one's spouse is no more applicable to the wife than to the husband and is best omitted. After the vows have been exchanged, it is preferable for the minister to pronounce the couple "husband and wife" (see Doctrine and Covenants 111:2c) rather than "man and wife" and

to introduce them to the congregation as "John and Jane Doe" rather than "Mr. and Mrs. John Doe."

4. Marriage is a relationship between two people that both creates a joint partnership and also preserves the identity of each spouse. Giving oneself to another in marriage is a commitment to sharing many things in common, but it also recognizes that the wife and husband will never and should never develop identical interests and capabilities in all things. The statement made by the minister in the wedding service should give attention to both of these dimensions of the relationship. This statement includes remarks directed to the couple and also remarks addressed to the congregation. The statement should be kept fairly brief.

5. Extravagance and luxury in any form is out of place in any service of worship. The wedding service is no exception. Floral arrangements, the dress of the wedding party, and the order of service itself should be dignified and all tendencies toward excess restrained.

6. Symbolism is an important aspect of all sacraments. The exchange of rings and the kiss are two acts that symbolize what happens in the wedding ceremony. Other such acts could include the exchange of other gifts, kissing or otherwise greeting the bride's and groom's parents, and the presentation to the couple of a special gift from the congregation.

Activities and Discussion Questions

1. Carefully analyze the prescribed part of the marriage ceremony (Doctrine and Covenants 111:2b). What does it mean to you? Which is the most important part? How would you express it in your

own words? Do you think any other statements should be included?

2. Discuss the meaning of the statement, "Marriage is ordained of God" (Doctrine and Covenants 49:3a). Does it mean that everyone should marry or that people who marry are exercising their discipleship more responsibly than those who don't? Read the explanatory statement at the beginning of Section 49.

3. Review the explanatory statement preceding the text of Doctrine and Covenants 111. Notice the words, "This section on marriage is not a revelation." Of what significance is this? Does it make its contents of less value than those of other sections of the Doctrine and Covenants?

4. Read the entire contents of Doctrine and Covenants 111 section by section. Discuss each paragraph in light of what is indicated on pages 113–115 above.

5. Why does the church accept marriages performed by other denominations when it does not accept their other sacraments? What would be the implication of the church *not* accepting such marriages?

6. What actually happens when two people are married? What does God do? What does the church do? What do the people being married do?

7. Why is it important that marriages be performed in a public ceremony? Does this have to be a worship service? What is wrong with a private ceremony?

8. What would be your advice to an RLDS member who was considering marrying someone of another faith? Why? Would you rather your son or daughter marry someone active in another faith or someone who claims no church affiliation? Why?

9. What are the purposes of marriage? What attitudes are appropriate toward couples who decide *not* to have children?
10. What is the meaning of the phrase, "for each other, and from all others" (Doctrine and Covenants 111:2b)? Exactly what, in your opinion, does this require? What does it prohibit?
11. If the church recognizes marriage by civil authority, what are the advantages of being married in the church?
12. What are the attractive features of a belief in marriage that continues beyond death? What problems are associated with this view?
13. Does it seem appropriate to you that people found guilty of adultery are to be expelled from the church if convicted a second time? Why or why not? What other offenses are serious enough to deserve expulsion?
14. Do you think it is appropriate to baptize polygamists into the church? Why or why not? What are legitimate grounds for denying a person membership in the church?
15. What accounts for the move in recent years to broaden the circumstances under which divorced people may remarry within the church? What effects does this have? Do you support the move?
16. What is the role of the single person in a church that stresses marriage strongly?
17. Reflect on your experiences of attending wedding ceremonies in other churches. What are the similarities and differences between the wedding practices of these churches and our own?

Notes

1. Doctrine and Covenants 49:3a (March 31, 1831).
2. Ibid., 108A:13 (in 1906 to 1952 editions; part of the preface in the 1970 and 1978 editions; eliminated in the 1990 edition).
3. Doctrine and Covenants C1, pages 251-252, in 1835 edition.
4. Doctrine and Covenants 111:1a.
5. Ibid., 111:1b.
6. Ibid., 111:1c.
7. Ibid.
8. See F. Henry Edwards, *The Edwards Commentary on the Doctrine and Covenants* (Independence, Missouri: Herald Publishing House, 1986), 397-398.
9. Doctrine and Covenants 111:2a-b.
10. Ibid., 111:2c.
11. Ibid., 111:2d.
12. Ibid., 111:3.
13. Ibid., 111:4a.
14. Ibid., 111:4b. See also 49:3b and 150:10a.
15. Ibid., 111:4b.
16. Genesis 2:18 KJV (2:23-24 IV). The IV reads, "And I, the Lord God, said unto mine Only Begotten, that it was not good that the man should be alone; wherefore, I will make an help meet for him."
17. Genesis 2:24 (2:30 IV).
18. Doctrine and Covenants 49:3a-c.
19. Ibid., 111:2c.
20. Matthew 19:6 and Mark 10:9 NRSV.
21. Doctrine and Covenants 111:2b.
22. Ibid.
23. See item 6 of this chapter for a discussion of divorce.
24. Matthew 16:19 KJV (16:20 IV); see also Matthew 18:18.
25. Matthew 22:30 KJV (22:29 IV); see also Mark 12:25 (12:29 IV) and Luke 20:35.
26. Doctrine and Covenants 111:2b; see also 42:7d.
27. Exodus 20, particularly verses 13-15.
28. Doctrine and Covenants 59:2c; see also 63:5a and 66:5e.
29. Ibid., 42:7e and 22a,b.
30. Ibid., 111:4a.
31. Ibid., 150:10a-b.
32. Ibid.
33. *Rules and Resolutions, 1990 Edition* (Independence, Missouri: Herald Publishing House, 1990), GCR 272 (adopted April 9, 1884).

34. Ibid., GCR 412 (adopted April 11, 1896).
35. Ibid., 1980 Edition, WCR 1034 (adopted April 6, 1962).
36. Ibid.
37. *Rules and Resolutions, 1990 Edition*, WCR 1182 (adopted April 6, 1984).

CHAPTER 8

The Evangelist's Blessing

The evangelist's blessing (formerly called patriarchal blessing) is a special blessing given by an evangelist. In tradition and purpose it is as old as Abraham, Isaac, and Jacob blessing their offspring[1] and Alma discerning his sons' needs and gifts, then offering them counsel and motivation.[2] In purpose it is related to the loving concern of Paul for Timothy as he urged him to stir up the gifts of God within him.[3]

The evangelist's blessing is given to people who are fifteen years of age and older at their request. Only one such blessing is given to each person. Bringing life into focus within the divine purpose and stimulating enlarged faith in God and commitment to Christ are inherent. Individuals receiving this blessing have testified to its benefits in sensing their potential, pulling the strands of life together, and lending through the years a steadying influence.

127

There is assurance of God's love and concern for the individual. There may be certain promises of God appropriate to that person's life, conditioned on the candidate's faithfulness. Evangelists testify that their own powers of observation are generally heightened in discernment. People are cautioned not to expect the future course of life to be foretold or decisions to be made for them. Rather, they are counseled to walk wisely, making decisions appropriate to their covenant with Christ.

Blessings may indicate, if the evangelist "feels so led," the "lineage" of the candidate. When this occurs, it is in terms of one of the twelve tribes of Israel, a reminder of one's heritage of faith and implying that qualities of life are to be developed appropriate to a people who sense keenly their relationship with God. Sometimes the validity or value of blessings has been thought of in terms of whether or not a lineage designation is included. This kind of comparison is, however, discouraged.[4] While designation of lineage was included in many blessings in earlier years, it has recently become more the exception than the rule.

The evangelist's blessing is intended to provide life-long guidance and support. A typed copy of the blessing is provided so the recipient can refer to it when in need of strength and guidance. The copy is made from a verbatim report taken in shorthand or by recording.

An individual desiring a blessing approaches a priest-hood member holding the office of evangelist. The candidate is advised to make preparation for the blessing by prayer, meditation, and the reading of a pamphlet prepared for the purpose of explaining the nature and intent of evangelist's blessings.

At the time scheduled for the blessing, the candidate and minister meet in a private room such as an office, chapel, or in a home. Sometimes, a place of natural beauty and quietness outdoors is chosen. The setting is one of worship, including scripture and prayer. Because of the intensely personal nature of the experience, no other individual is present with the possible exception of a stenographer who records the blessing.

Throughout the Restoration the significance of the evangelist's blessing has been suggested by the fact that a copy is kept on file and available in case the original is lost. The person may receive a copy of the blessing by writing to the office of the presiding evangelist.

Origin and Historical Development

Patriarchal blessings were first given in the Latter Day Saint Church by Joseph Smith, Sr., who was ordained to the office of patriarch by his son, Joseph Smith, Jr., on December 18, 1833, at Kirtland, Ohio.[5] Joseph Smith, Sr., gave blessings to his children and to other persons in the church.[6] In those days the concept of a single lifelong patriarchal blessing was not defined and so some people received more than one blessing. From available evidence it appears that blessings were more specific in terms of a person's lineage and future.[7]

Joseph Smith, Sr.'s blessings of the members of the First Presidency were accompanied by the anointing of their heads with oil.[8] It is not known how widespread this practice was.

Early in the Latter Day Saint movement, the concept of lineage was important in the determination of who held the patriarchal office. When one traces the concepts of the patriarchal blessing and of the office of patriarch back to the Old Testament patriarchs, it is understandable how lineage became a concern of Joseph Smith, Jr., and of the church. Following the death of Joseph Smith, Sr., in 1840, his son Hyrum was appointed as his successor. In making this designation, Joseph Smith, Jr., indicated that, "my servant Hyrum may take the office of priesthood and patriarch, which was appointed unto him by his father, by blessing and also by right."[9] Concern over this matter of lineage accounted in part for the Reorganization having no patriarch until Alexander Smith was designated "patriarch to the church"[10] in 1897. Lineage no longer plays a significant role in the calling and ordination of people to this office.

In 1835 direction came to the church that "It is the duty of the Twelve, in all large branches of the church, to ordain evangelical ministers, as they shall be designated unto them by revelation."[11] The extent to which this provision was implemented in the early church is not clear. It is reasonable to conclude, however, that the number of patriarchal blessings given was somewhat limited.

In 1901 President Joseph Smith III delivered inspired instruction to the church regarding the role of patriarchs in the church.[12] In that same year several additional patriarchs were ordained. From that time on the number of patriarchs has increased. The Order of Evangelists now numbers over 500. The ordination of additional members to this office has provided the church with the benefit of their various ministries, including, but not limited to, blessings.[13] The calling of additional patriarchs led to the designation in 1903 of a "Presiding Patriarch."[14]

Throughout much of the twentieth century the terms "patriarch," "evangelist-patriarch," and "evangelist" have been used interchangeably. However, until recently, the blessing has been referred to consistently as "patriarchal blessing." The adoption of the term "evangelist" as the preferred designation and description of the blessing as the "evangelist's blessing" are emerging as more appropriate in an age when the office is held by women as well as men. This is confirmed by the designation of Paul W. Booth as "Presiding Evangelist" in 1992,[15] coming as a departure from the tradition of most of his predecessors in the office as presiding patriarch.[16]

Activities and Discussion Questions

1. Ask an evangelist to explain the nature of evangelist's blessings and to answer any questions you may have.
2. Obtain a copy of the latest pamphlet on evangelist's blessings and read the entire contents. Discuss the various sections in a group setting.
3. Why is only one blessing given to a person?
4. What do you see as the most important function of an evangelist's blessing? What happens to the candidate as a result of the blessing?
5. In a practical sense, how can an evangelist's blessing be most helpful to a person? If you have received such a blessing, how has it been helpful to you?
6. Why are evangelist's blessings given in private? Should candidates be allowed to have anyone they choose present for the blessing? Why or why not?
7. What would be the advantages and disadvantages of evangelist's blessings being given in a public worship setting?
8. What kinds of times in a person's life would be most appropriate to receive one's evangelist's blessing?

9. What similarities do you see between the practice of a father blessing his sons in the Old Testament and the present-day practice of giving evangelist's blessings?
10. Why do you suppose that evangelist's blessings were sometimes accompanied by anointing with oil? What purpose would this serve?
11. Why do you suppose evangelist's blessings are available only to members of the RLDS Church? Do you agree with this policy? Why or why not?

Notes

1. Genesis 27, 48, and 49; Doctrine and Covenants 83:2e.
2. Alma 17, 18, and 19.
3. II Timothy 1:6.
4. For a more extensive discussion of the designation of lineage in patriarchal blessings, see *The Patriarchs* edited by Reed M. Holmes (Independence, Missouri: Herald Publishing House, 1978), 122-129.
5. "A Brief History of Patriarchal Ministry in the Restoration, Part I" by Richard P. Howard, *Saints Herald* 122, no. 8 (August 1975): 28. Reprinted in *The Patriarchs*, 20-39.
6. Copies of some of the blessings given by Joseph Smith, Sr., are in the RLDS Church Library-Archives in Independence, Missouri.
7. See blessing of Abel Butterfield (December 8, 1836), reprinted in part in Richard Howard, op. cit., 22.
8. *History of the Church of Jesus Christ of Latter Day Saints*, Volume II (Salt Lake City, Utah: Deseret News, 1904). Joseph Smith, Jr., also anointed his father when ordaining him earlier on the same occasion.
9. Doctrine and Covenants 107:29b. (Removed from Appendix by World Conference action in 1990.)
10. Ibid., 124:2a. Following Hyrum Smith's death in 1844, his younger brother, William, served as patriarch for about one year, giving more than 300 blessings. Additional information on the circumstances in the early Reorganization can be found in Richard Howard's article cited in note 5.
11. Ibid., 104:17.
12. Ibid., 125:3-6.
13. See "A List of Readings on Patriarchs" (mimeographed paper), prepared by the RLDS Library-Archives in Independence, Missouri.
14. See Doctrine and Covenants 125:5a.
15. Ibid., 158:3.
16. Ibid., 125:5a, 130:3b, 145:4, 151:2, and 155:2. Note the exception where Elbert A. Smith was not so designated when called to preside over the Order of Evangelists in 1938. See Ibid., 137:4.

CHAPTER 9

Administration to the Sick

The sacrament of administration is based on the New Testament accounts of Jesus and others healing sick people. According to the Gospel accounts, Jesus healed a ruler's daughter, blind persons, a dumb man, a centurion's servant, a leper, a paralytic, and many others.[1] Not only did Jesus heal individuals himself, he also indicated that such power would be granted to those who believed in him.[2] Peter is recorded as healing a lame man at the temple gate.[3]

In James is found the admonition, "Are any among you sick? They should call for the elders of the church and have them pray over them, anointing them with oil in the name of the Lord."[4] This statement forms the basis for the current practice of administration in the RLDS Church. First, administration is by elders. Second, the elders shall pray for the sick person. Third, they shall anoint the sick person with oil. A fourth dimension is the use of the laying on of hands. This is indicated in the Doctrine and Covenants as follows: "And the elders of the church, two or more, shall be called, and shall pray for, and lay their hands upon them [the sick] in my name."[5]

Healing is referred to in the Book of Mormon also. We read there that Jesus and his disciples healed various sick people.[6]

The sacrament of administration is available to RLDS members and other people alike. Someone who is physically, emotionally, or in any other way sick may request administration. The elders take with them a small vial of olive oil that has already been consecrated for the purpose of administration. Consecration takes the form of an elder offering prayer over the open vial specifying the purpose for which it is to be used. The oil is not reconsecrated each time it is used.

The sacrament of administration is performed in this way: one of the elders anoints the head of the candidate with a drop of oil and, laying his hands on the candidate's head, offers a short prayer or statement. This may include the invoking of God's Spirit and presence on the occasion and contain admonition to the candidate to have faith in God. Following the anointing, the second elder adds his hands to the candidate's head and offers the prayer of petition or confirmation. The focus of this prayer is the presenting of the sick person to God for whatever blessing might be forthcoming. Although there may be a natural desire for those officiating to request or even promise the recovery of the candidate to good health, this practice is discouraged as "a fruitful source of trouble among my people."[7]

On occasions where only one elder is available this sacrament may be administered by the elder doing both the anointing and confirming. If another person is present, he or she is sometimes asked to offer prayer before the anointing.

Administration is usually done in the privacy of a person's home, office, or hospital room. In these situations one or more friends or relatives may be present. On occasion, however, administration may be performed in a church sanctuary following a service of worship while other people are present or even as part of a formal service of worship. Such would be the case if it was considered appropriate by the candidate and officiating ministers.

The purpose of administration is to provide the sick person with assurance of God's care and concern and also of the church's interest in that person. It is also to seek a blessing and alleviate fear and pain. The result of any particular blessing, of course, cannot be predicted. Some people have testified of receiving miraculous healings while others have shown no tangible evidence of improvement. Reorganized Latter Day Saints are not "faith healers" in the sense that they believe that healing will necessarily occur if a person has sufficient faith. Faith is, however, an important element in administration.[8] When a person approaches the sacrament in the spirit of prayer and faith, it is customary for that person to be blessed in some meaningful way. For this reason individual preparation is emphasized. It is important that the person understand the purpose and significance of administration and approach it in a spirit of humble anticipation.

The Gospels frequently record Jesus as associating healing with forgiveness of sin. A key example is in the Matthew account of Jesus healing the man with palsy.[9] Also, in the letter of James, we find, "And the prayer of faith shall save the sick, and the Lord shall raise him up; and if he have committed sins, they shall be forgiven him."[10] In RLDS practice the forgiveness of sin is sometimes associated with healing but is not as dominant a theme as it was in New Testament times when it was usual to assume that sickness resulted directly from sin.

At times administration is referred to as the sacrament of *healing*. If healing is understood in the broad sense as any physical, emotional, or psychological benefit, then the term is applicable. But if by the use of the term "healing" it is implied that particular kinds of sicknesses will necessarily be alleviated as a direct result of administration, then the use of the term is ill-advised.

Administration is most appropriately seen in the context of a broad concern for wholeness and health. This involves spiritual, mental, and emotional well-being as well as physical health. Wholeness also extends beyond one's individual life to relationships with God and other people. In a world in which fragmentation is the dominant life experience for many people, the church points to the need for development of integrated lives with balanced expressions of the various aspects of personhood. Administration is an important symbol and expression of God's and the church's concern for people as whole beings.[11]

The sacrament of administration asserts the role of the church as *one* agent (or channel) of God's healing ministry. It does not deny that healing occurs through other channels. The church has always maintained that administration should occur along with the treatment of sickness by normal medical procedures. Neither does the church assert that healing will definitely occur as the result of administration. Referring to those who have received administration, the Doctrine and Covenants says, "If they die, they shall die unto me, and if they live, they shall live unto me."[12]

Activities and Discussion Questions

1. The sacrament of administration is sometimes referred to as "healing." What does this imply? Do you think this term is appropriate? Why or why not?

2. What is the role of the consecrated oil in administration? Why is it consecrated? What happens in administration that requires the use of the oil? Would the administration be in some sense invalid if the oil were not consecrated or if no oil were used? Is the oil symbolic? If so, what does it symbolize?

3. What actually happens during administration? How are people different than they were before the administration?

4. Why is the laying on of hands used in administration? What does it symbolize?

5. What are the similarities and differences between the church's current practice of administration and the biblical accounts of Jesus, his disciples, and early church figures performing acts of healing? Read the biblical verses listed in references 1-10 as the basis for discussion.

6. What is the relationship between sickness and sin and between forgiving sin and healing sickness?

7. How would you explain administration to a non-RLDS friend who is skeptical about it?

8. What do you see as the relationship between administration and the help that people can receive from physicians and other health-care professionals?

9. What are the reasons for making administration available to people who are not members of the RLDS Church? Do you agree with them? Do you believe that administration is more effective for people who are RLDS than for those who are not? Why or why not?

10. Give examples of the various kinds of sicknesses for which administration might provide ministry. Are there situations when you think requests for administration should be refused? If so, what situations?

11. Should administration be available as frequently as a person requests it? What are its possible abuses? How can they be avoided?

12. If you were explaining administration to someone other than an RLDS member who was about to receive it, what would you say?

13. What preparation (a) by the elders who will perform the sacrament, and (b) by the one being administered to is appropriate for administration?

14. Is it appropriate to talk about the "success" of administration? What "results" can reasonably be expected? If "nothing happens," then should one "try again"?

15. Do you think it is appropriate for administrations to be held in a church sanctuary during or after a service of worship? Why or why not?

16. Read Doctrine and Covenants 42:12-13 carefully. What does it say about the role of faith and of the laying on of hands?

Notes

1. See, for example, Matthew 9, Mark 5, and Luke 7 and 8.
2. Mark 16:18 (16:19 IV); and Mormon 4:87.
3. Acts 3:1-8.
4. James 5:14 NRSV.
5. Doctrine and Covenants 42:12d.
6. III Nephi 8:9 and IV Nephi 1:6; see also Alma 10:100 and Mormon 4:87.
7. Doctrine and Covenants 125:15a.
8. See Ibid., 42:12-13.
9. Matthew 9:2-8 (9:2-9 IV), Mark 2:3-12 (2:3-9 IV), and Luke 5:17-26.
10. James 5:15.
11. Doctrine and Covenants 156:5c.
12. Ibid., 42:12d.